Rediscovering Your Happily Ever After

Moving from Hopeless to Hopeful as a Newly Divorced Mother

PeggySue Wells

D0967633

Kregel
Publications

Rediscovering Your Happily Ever After: Moving from Hopeless to Hopeful as a Newly Divorced Mother

© 2010 by PeggySue Wells

Published by Kregel Publications, a division of Kregel, Inc., P.O. Box 2607, Grand Rapids, MI 49501.

ISBN 978-0-8254-3930-8

Printed in the United States of America
10 11 12 13 14 / 5 4 3 2 1

To my favorite children:
AmyRose, Leilani, Holly, Josiah,
Estee, Hannah, and Lilyanna.

To insightful Chris Matthews,
who invited me to play full out;
to gentle Toby Fisher and his hooey alarm;
to accepting Cecelia Esposito, who helped me
make choices; and to supportive Thad Wells,
who shares a similar journey. Thanks for asking
for my heart and not settling for anything less.

CONTENTS

CONTENTS

ACKNOWLEDGMENTS

Heartfelt thanks to Mary Ann Froehlich, my cherished friend and fellow author, who explored the topic of forgiveness with me both academically and practically. To dear and authentic Pat Palau, who faced her fear head-on and left footprints for me to follow. To Saundra Stephenson, who taught me about *Him*possibilities.

Writing is a team sport and I am grateful for my winning team: talented and refreshingly opinionated agent Chip MacGregor, insightful editor Dawn Anderson, and the folks at Kregel Publications who shared the vision for this project.

ONCE UPON A TIME

Note to self:
Wheels on luggage do not work on sand.

It stinks. Standing at ground zero, mourning the loss of a marriage stinks. God designed marriage to be a lifelong covenant. A cord of three strands: you, your spouse, and the Lord. That's plan A. There is no plan B.

But many find themselves here. Statistics tell us that more than 50 percent of marriages end in divorce. The numbers are staggering enough; when you put the faces of men, women, and precious children in place of those numbers, the heartbreak and devastation is criminal.

Countless books describe how to save troubled marriages. I have read many of them. Plenty of books debate when and if separation and divorce are permitted in the eyes of God. I'll leave those topics to those experts. This book is for people who, like it or not—and none of us like it—find themselves in the debris, mourning the death of a marriage.

Singer Stevie Nicks said in her song titled "Landslide" that she was afraid of making life changes because she'd built her life around one key person. Many of us can relate. Suddenly, the person we orbited is no longer the center of our universe. Dazed and confused, we look around wondering how to put the world back together, and feel pretty clueless about where to begin. Shell-shocked, we find it difficult to focus when we most need to. We may not have wanted change but now change has been thrust upon us. It is time for a course adjustment.

In the midst of this life-altering upheaval, you may feel as I did— abandoned by God. My heavenly bridegroom, my heavenly father. Moving from being an *us* to being me, and a new me at that, was confusing, frustrating, and frightening. When I most needed to know God was beside me, holding my hand and leading me through the dark, I felt like he, too, had deserted me.

The good news is that God is still God of all creation. He created you and you are valued. In the midst of unbelievable betrayal, God promised to use even this horrific chapter of your life. In his unequaled economy, nothing, not even this, goes to waste. He'll help you navigate this huge upheaval. Though it feels like an eternity, the emotional agony is for a season. As absurd as it may sound, joy will return if you are willing to move forward.

This book is an extra large scoop of hope. You'll discover, as I did, that whatever is over our heads is under God's feet. Whatever seems impossible is actually *Him*possible.

> We ask ourselves, Who am I to be brilliant, gorgeous, talented, fabulous? Actually, who are you not to be? You are a child of God. Your playing small does not serve the world.
>
> MARIANNE WILLIAMSON, *A RETURN TO LOVE*

CHAPTER 1

TUMBLING DOWN THE RABBIT HOLE

How do I find my way?

I hate the conflict that shadows my house.
I hate the suffocating smog of lies. I hate the hate that
reigns in power. I hate the heat that scorches the life
out of everything. I wish one breath of sweet, fresh air
would just once brush my cheek. And such would be
just one thought of honesty.

MY DAUGHTER

Where's Dad's car?"
Peering out the windows of our fifteen-passenger van, my daughter searched the driveway. In the back, the chatter of the other children abruptly quieted. At the end of the long gravel lane, our house was strangely dark.

I parked and turned off the engine. The children piled out and in anxious silence made their way into the house while I unstrapped the toddler from her car seat. Inside, the older children turned on lights.

Taking the steps two at a time, my son raced upstairs to the master bedroom. With the baby on my hip, I followed.

He met me at the top of the stairs. The light from my bathroom was still on behind him. "Dad's toothbrush isn't here."

"He left." My daughter leaned against the wall and slid to the floor.

Another daughter went to her father's medicine chest to look inside. Then she went to the clothes closet. "He's gone," she said.

I dropped onto the edge of the bed and the younger children buried themselves in my lap. We held each other while my oldest children collapsed on the carpet and sobbed.

Weeks earlier, following years of counseling that failed to curtail an escalating situation, our family had gathered in the family room. "You either have to stop being abusive or find another place to live," I told my husband. "It's not good for you to treat me this way. It's not good for me to be treated this way. It isn't good for my son to think this is how men treat women, and it's not good for the girls to think this is how men treat women."

He chose to leave.

Now I looked at my beloved children, their lovely faces reflecting the wrenching pain of their broken hearts. How could I ease their devastation? Where does the wounded caretaker go to be cared for? Where was God? What do I do now?

Initially after their dad left, the children and I felt marked relief. The tension was gone. We could relax and eat again. The first six months I did double duty trying to keep all of life's many plates spinning, to provide stability for the children and their understandably confused emotions, all the while holding onto hope that he'd get himself together and return home.

The children and I were humiliated that we were now what society termed a broken home. We were embarrassed that we had not been enough to inspire him to love us and make the effort to be a family with us.

"Why don't you just start over? Start the relationship fresh and build it," one child had suggested to him a year earlier.

"You don't understand," he replied. "It's too hard."

It was six months before each of the children tentatively told someone in their circle that their dad was no longer part of our household.

I operated in crisis mode, working overtime to help the children adjust while dodging the unkind behavior of the man who once promised before God, family, and friends to love and cherish me. The principles our family was built on were torn away like a storm-tossed ship whose ties to the dock were severed. I kept waiting for things to settle down. But they never did.

Years later, for my birthday, my teenage son gave me a George Strait CD. This multi–award winning country singer recorded a song titled *She Let Herself Go* that my son wanted me to hear. The words he penned on the accompanying card read, "Sometimes you just gotta let yourself go and get a life."

I was a long way from thriving. Barely surviving was a more accurate description, and that wasn't good for me or for my children. Like the song said, it was time to let myself go and get a life. For all of our sakes. It was time to make changes and make them right away.

Welcome to your new beginning. Finding yourself unintentionally single is doubtless not the life you had expected. Standing in the shattered pieces of your hoped-for happily ever after, it's time to rise like a phoenix from the relationship ashes and begin living again.

You have a huge hole in your heart. People say that time heals all wounds. While waiting for my gaping injury to heal, I discovered that God often prefers not to eliminate the hole but teaches us to live with it. And then he artfully weaves it into the fabric of life. In his economy, he will use even this.

We can facilitate the process. When we are wounded, it is tempting to cocoon. To draw a tight circle and stay inside the safety of that comfortable, familiar, and controlled zone. To become the incredible shrinking violet. But healing and life exist outside the walls we build around our hearts. I dare you to plug your nose and dive headfirst into the rushing river of God's grace, forgiveness, and love.

Five steps took me forward. These were simple acts I could incorporate by noon. A simple attitude adjustment that is reaping a lifetime of benefits. For me and for those dear to me. Surprisingly, these steps also helped me look more beautiful—inside and out. Even my posture improved.

 You are not big steps away from anything; you are small shifts away from everything.

Keith Kochner

It was time to make some shifts. I was ready for some shifty days.

1. Stop blaming.

As long as I continued to blame others for the situation, I stayed stuck. Whether I blamed my husband, my parents, or myself, the blame only kept me cemented in the same spot.

The same is true for all of us. Are we blaming a husband, in-laws, or the other woman? Blame cripples only one person. Me. It has no effect on the target of my blame. That other person is not sitting at home wringing his hands because I am convinced that my circumstances are his fault. That other person is living life while I resemble Winnie the Pooh's gloomy, gray, albeit cute, friend Eeyore.

Does that mean my spouse is no longer responsible for his behavior? Does it mean that you or I were not treated abysmally? Or that I wasn't hurt?

Certainly not. The hurt, pain, betrayal, and devastation are real. Fact.

 A man can fail many times but he isn't a failure until he begins to blame someone else.

John Burroughs

However, by playing the blame game, those facts became my excuses for not moving forward. Freedom came when I acknowledged the truth of the situation. People made choices. I made choices. He made choices. Some of those choices hurt me deeply. Some of those choices made a Grand Canyon–sized impact on my life.

Now, what choices was I going to make today?

A friend or counselor who allows us to vent, to cry and scream about our pain, is a gift. Initially, when all we feel is the betrayal, a tender listening ear can help us express our grief and verbally process.

"How are you?" My brother telephoned from out of state. His question was rooted in common courtesy and he expected the customary, "Fine, thanks. And you?"

"Some days," I confided, "it hurts so bad I can't breathe."

Curled in the fetal position and crying for days is a common experience for those in this situation. But camping there, the pain became my identity. When I spoke at a national conference, an attendee asked me to look at her résumé before she submitted it to a potential boss. Rather than listing her education and professional experience, she spent paragraphs explaining that she was divorced but had since made peace with her ex-spouse. Being divorced and the pain surrounding that chapter in her life had become her résumé.

I've seen the same in women's groups, both professional and social. For many women, it doesn't take long before they share they are abandoned by their husbands, divorced, rejected, and now struggling to be a single parent. Ironically, men in similar situations rarely confide such details. Just picturing it is laughable. It may be part of their history but it is not their address.

Certainly the demands of motherhood are topics we share with friends and family. For both single and married moms, there are days when life's challenges are more intense than others. Yet there is a vast difference between dealing with today's concerns and claiming a card-carrying permanent victim status of divorce.

In many breakups, one spouse is eager to move on to a new life. For that person who emotionally left the relationship some time before, the divorce is a tedious hurdle. For those of us who dreamed of living happily ever after, we can stumble through the process quite wounded. For me, this was not how I thought my life or my wedding vows would turn out. I couldn't accept that the person I gave my life, love, body, and future to could treat me so callously. I got stuck in my pain. And bitterness.

Recovery began when I limited the amount of time I spent in this place. A day of crying. Ten minutes of venting on the phone. A lunch date with a friend. An hour with a counselor. Permit yourself seven paces. Seven paces to mentally beat yourself up. This principle allows us to grieve, to cry, and to feel our broken heart. To blame myself or someone else for the situation.

Then we must begin to step out of it. Give up our hope for a better past. Face the reality of the present and make choices that move our lives forward. I'd rather be traveling through the sand on my way to the Promised Land than be perpetually camped in the stinking desert.

It happened.

So what?

Now what?

 Be not a slave to your own past. Plunge into the sublime seas, dive deep, and swim far, so that you shall come back with self-respect, with new power, with an advanced experience, that shall explain and overlook the old.

Ralph Waldo Emerson

Looking Glass: Do you regularly offer excuses? If you show up late at a place and waste further time by blaming your lateness on the kids, the dog, or the traffic, you are playing the blame game. You are blaming someone or something else for your situation.

The only person who believes your excuse is you. When you are late, it is apparent that you did not plan your time to arrive at least fifteen minutes early in case you were delayed by life.

In the military, fifteen minutes early is on time. On time is late. Soldiers quickly learn that there are only four acceptable responses—yes, sir; no, sir; I don't understand, sir; and no excuse, sir.

When I dropped making excuses, my days and relationships streamlined. Free from cumbersome excuses, my conversations improved. People are attracted to those who fully live life without excuses.

2. Release others from your expectations.

Repeatedly doing the same thing but each time expecting different results is the description of insanity. Expecting someone who has continually treated me poorly to suddenly treat me with honor and respect is going to disappoint only one person. Me.

Expecting an irresponsible individual to act responsibly today is sure to prove frustrating. Certainly, people can choose to make good choices. We hope and pray that they will. It was the expectation that tripped me up. I had to allow other people the freedom to be who they are by releasing them from my expectations. It's what I want them to do for me.

I had a neighbor who telephoned only to complain. Initially, I greeted each call with enthusiasm, looking forward to building a neighborly relationship. But every encounter was a tirade of criticism. No matter how often I adjusted our lifestyle to please my neighbor, the disapproval continued. After several months of this pattern, I no longer expected us to become friends. I released my neighbor from my expectations.

Surprisingly, I spent years expecting that *this time* my spouse would treat me honorably. Even after he left, I held high hopes that he would reverse his choices. Though I only invested months in expecting my neighbor to be a pleasant addition to my life, I held onto higher expectations for my spouse for decades. Long after patterns showed me he was not going to be what I anticipated him to be, I continued to clutch my expectations close. I created excuses for his actions and denied reality.

Letting go of my assumptions of how I thought he should behave, of how I thought he should treat me, was a healthy step forward. Stepping back and taking an honest look at who this person really was based on his consistent behavior was a hearty dose of honesty. When I finally took off my rose-colored expectation spectacles, I no longer left each phone call and encounter perpetually hurt because my high hopes were not fulfilled.

If someone in your life has a history of being inconsiderate, don't look for him or her to be concerned about your feelings. If your aunt is consistently malicious, I doubt she will suddenly morph into Miss Personality Plus at the next family reunion. If your spouse withheld money, affection, or respect before, he's sure to do the same now. If he didn't treat you well before, don't think he will do so today.

Release your spouse from your dream of happily ever after. When you release others, you are set free from unhealthy patterns, disappointments, excuse making, and the exhausting effort of living in denial. The person you set free is you.

Looking Glass: If you are thinking *maybe this time* about anyone, it is a signal that you are clutching onto expectations you have about that person. Expectations regarding how you believe that person should act, behave, or feel.

If you are regularly offended, it is a sure sign that you're harboring rigid assumptions. It is time to release that person from your expectations and allow them the freedom to be who they truly are.

3. Channel your anger constructively.

One woman said she smashed her husband's windshield. Carrie Underwood sang a song in a minor key about a woman who destroyed her lover's new, souped-up four-wheel drive when she caught him cheating. Could I relate? Yeah!

I actually chastised myself for being too cowardly to vent my anger toward him. But there was no lack of anger and the associated adrenaline. Being livid at being hurt and betrayed is normal. Anger is not a sin. Ephesians 4:26 instructs, "In your anger do not sin." Marcus Aurelius said, "How much more grievous are the consequences of anger than the causes of it."

Anger is a gift from God. It is an emotion that recognizes a wrong and empowers us to do something about it. What we choose to do with our anger makes a big difference in our ability to move forward. What we do with the anger can be either sinful or productive. "No man can think clearly when his fists are clenched," said drama critic George Jean Nathan.

When Cari Lightner was killed by a drunk driver with a record for driving while drunk, her mother was angry. Candace Lightner channeled her fury in a healthy direction. Candace founded Mothers Against Drunk Driving. MADD has had a positive impact nationwide. Candace will never know this side of heaven how many lives she saved by channeling her anger constructively and initiating stronger laws against drunk driving and repeat offenders. You and I may have been positively affected by this mother's diligent efforts.

"For we know him who said, 'It is mine to avenge; I will repay'" (Heb. 10:30). The Lord has given us instructions in the face of mistreatment:

> Is not this the kind of fasting I have chosen: to loose the chains of injustice and untie the cords of the yoke, to set the oppressed free and break every yoke? Is it not to share your food with the hungry and to provide the poor wanderer with shelter—when you see the naked, to clothe him, and not to turn away from your own flesh and blood? Then your light will break forth like the dawn, and your healing will quickly

appear; then your righteousness will go before you, and the glory of the LORD will be your rear guard. Then you will call, and the LORD will answer; you will cry for help, and he will say: Here am I. If you do away with the yoke of oppression, with the pointing finger and malicious talk, and if you spend yourselves in behalf of the hungry and satisfy the needs of the oppressed, then your light will rise in the darkness, and your night will become like the noonday. (Isaiah 58:6–10)

One woman rolled up her sleeves, harnessed her adrenaline, and tackled all the neglected chores around the house. She replaced a leaky window, fixed a shower, changed out old carpet, updated paint, and hauled away trash. She created a lovely environment.

Another woman started a support group for single moms. She compiled a list of agencies that offered services for mothers and children. She planned monthly meetings where the ladies studied the Bible. These women traded skills. One exchanged babysitting with another who knew how to wallpaper. They helped do each other's taxes. They spruced up each other's yards, cried on each other's shoulders, and cheered for each other's children.

Many women channel their energy into completing a college degree. When I returned to college, half the class consisted of traditional students working on their degree right after high school. The other half was made up of women of my vintage. Though a few were empty nesters, most were getting equipped to take care of themselves and their children.

Plenty of single women decide to dust off old dreams. They start businesses, go to work in their field of interest, partner with philanthropic organizations, and hone their hobbies from painting to music to writing. One lady opened a stylish interior design store. Two ladies opened an upscale bakeshop serving the community and shipping delicious treats nationwide. Three gals became family physicians. Another woman organized mission trips to third world countries where teams of women brought medical clinics and support to poor women and their children. "For we are God's workmanship, created in Christ Jesus to do good works, which God prepared in advance for us to do" (Eph. 2:10).

In my experience, women who continue to blame and vent their anger unconstructively become bitter and contentious individuals. It is "better to dwell in the wilderness, than with a contentious and angry woman," warns Proverbs 21:19 (NKJV). I can be bitter and contentious or I can be gentle, gracious, and productive. The choice is mine.

Looking Glass: Are you laughing or are you a fun-sucker? Angry people who are not using their anger and adrenaline to create something positive suck the fun right out of any room or group they enter. Despite the anger that pain and betrayal generate, are you creating something worthy of your time and energy? If you're not laughing frequently, you are a fun-sucker.

4. Embrace healthy relationships and maintain a distance from toxic ones.

Are you collecting ministry projects? If your circle of friends consists solely of people who need to be rescued, and individuals who join you in poor-me pity parties, it's time to expand your circle.

My relationships are healthiest when they include someone I mentor, my peers, and someone who mentors me. Healthy relationships do not allow me to perpetually be the victim, nor do they drain me dry with their own insatiable needs.

I sometimes fear becoming too vulnerable in a friendship because I fear being rejected. I fear competition. I don't want to appear to be needy.

Completeness comes first through our relationship with God. Good friends encourage us to be the best we can be. They don't buy our excuses for staying stuck. Develop a plan with the counsel of those who hold a similar heart. Begin with God and wisely add others with unselfish motivations. That's how change happens.

Healthy friendships can say no to each other and remain strong. Healthy friendships share feelings honestly and can trust each other to honor confidences. These associations are accountable, available, and give each other freedom to fail—as we all will on occasion. Healthy friendships are built on equal footing and they ask each other about progress on their goals.

Healthy friendships are not always there or everlasting. They can be seasonal. Only Jesus Christ is our forever friend. Healthy friendships are not competitive, envious, exclusive, rescuing, smothering, or testing.

 Never approach a bull from the front, a horse from the rear, or a fool from any direction.

Cowboy wisdom

Looking Glass: What motivates you to be someone's friend? Do you like yourself for who God created you to be? Or are you seeking fulfillment from another? Are you drawn to people because of your common pain? Or do you relate to their greatness, potential, and the opportunity to participate together in society?

When you like yourself, rejection will still be disappointing, but not overpowering. Scripture tells us that God loves and accepts us. You and I are beautiful in the eyes of the Lord. When we choose to believe God's word, rejection from others no longer devastates or destroys us.

Accepting yourself includes . . .

Accepting that Christ loves you enough to die for you
Being content with your age
Being content with your weight
Developing your talents

Not sabotaging your potential

Working with your limitations and not taking on more than you are able

 Oh, the comfort—the inexpressible comfort of feeling safe with a person—having neither to weigh thoughts, nor measure words, but pouring them all right out, just as they are, chaff and grain together; certain that a faithful hand will take and sift them, keep what is worth keeping, and then with the breath of kindness blow the rest away.

Dinah Craik, *A Life for a Life*

I am involved with healthy relationships when my friends and I both dream big and accomplish our goals. We support and encourage each other to be our best.

5. Take responsibility for yourself.

This is the single most important step toward positive change.

For too long I relied on others to care for me. I relied on my parents and my husband for emotional and financial support. Even when it was substandard, I expected these emotional and physical needs to be supplied by another person. Like a character in Jane Austen's *Sense and Sensibility*, or *Pride and Prejudice*, I viewed a husband as my financial plan.

Often, after the breakup of a marriage, women settle for second best in life because that is what is left to them. Financial support may be minimal but we make do with it. I was an expert at accepting lemons I shouldn't have accepted in the first place and then I knocked myself out making them into lemonade. I was an expert at being a victim.

Do you have an excuse and a story for everything? The victim mentality is characterized by explanations and justifications. The conversation of a perpetual victim is focused on how bad things are, how someone else has done them wrong, and the unending list of reasons why they can't do something. They sound like a bad country western song.

The victim mentality is easy to put on. There are generous perks to being a victim. We wouldn't adopt the victim mentality if there weren't benefits.

Ouch. I hated discovering that being a victim was not something someone else did to me but something I did to myself.

When I'm a victim, I can be self-centered, focused on all the hard things that happened in my life. I get to recite my ever-lengthening list of wrongs that have been perpetrated on me to gain sympathy from others subjected to my tale of woe. Occasionally, a codependent type will respond by helping me in some way and I feel validated.

Being a victim means I don't have to succeed or achieve my full potential. I can carve out a mediocre comfort level similar to the dip in an old mattress, and stay there. I always have justification for sabotaging my dreams, dropping out of programs and projects, and not quite becoming a professional or succeeding at anything. I run a lot of 99-yard dashes instead of finishing the 100-yard run.

Best of all, being a victim means I place responsibility for myself on someone else. I can expect others to take care of me and then whine about how my needs have not been met. It becomes a perpetuating cycle of being a victim so I am victimized so I am a victim so I am victimized.

The victim mentality is tough to remove because it's self-inflicted. It's the single greatest contributor to staying stuck and living below the abundant life God promised. To stop being a victim, I had to stop blaming others and genuinely face myself. I had to acknowledge the ways I participated in the situation. Certainly some situations clearly have one party who violated major agreements in a relationship. But how I contributed, ignored, denied, enabled, and responded are entirely mine to own. If I complain that I had no voice in the financial arena, I also have to acknowledge that I allowed that to occur.

Larry Burkett said men abuse because they can. The message here is that people—male and female—will do what others allow them to do.

The only one who makes me a victim is me. The only one who can change that in me is me. I had to look at myself and see what I'd denied about myself. It was time to see what others had seen all along. I had to put on surgical gloves, dig deep, and make repairs.

The terrifying aspect of this step was accepting responsibility for the results. Accepting that success was up to me. I also own my failures. Me. Not anyone else. I chose to no longer accept lemons from others. I chose to no longer accept lemons from myself. Moving from victim to personally responsible meant, like the sign President Truman posted on his desk when he made the decision to drop the nuclear bomb, "The buck stops here."

But it's more than worth the effort to move from victim to victorious. It's worth it to face our fears about being personally responsible and plunge into the abundant life that God promised. Even if you've never done it before, you can become a big girl, a mature woman who is responsible for yourself.

It's not terribly difficult. The change in attitude can be implemented in moments. The Lord frees us when we partner with him to become personally responsible for our spiritual, mental, emotional, physical, sexual, and financial well-being. Suddenly the world is transformed from a series of all the things we can't have or can't do to a vast universe overflowing with potential and possibilities. We can make choices. We can find solutions. We can make mistakes and learn from them. We can suffer legitimate victimization without remaining a victim. No longer a ball and chain, the past becomes a stepping stone to a promising future.

Our faith grows when we stop relying on another human being, or the government, or the church to take care of our needs. No other person will ever be our savior. When we embrace responsibility for our own happiness, health, future, and provision, we lean more on Jehovah Jirah, our God who declares that he is our provision. Our conversation is positive, centered on others, ideas, and possibilities. People enjoy our company and appreciate partnering with us because we bring optimism, steadfastness, and faithfulness to relationships and projects. We attract friends who make a lasting impact on the world.

My happiness and situation in life are, in large part, determined by my own choices. There are benefits and prices to every action that I choose. It is vital that I weigh the cost and the perk of each decision and then take action. When I find myself making poor choices, the truth is that I am receiving some benefit from this decision that presently outweighs choosing a different option. Ouch again.

Continual frustration is a sign that I'm out of sync with God's plan. A personal retreat is a vehicle for getting on track with what the Lord has already created for me to do. A conference center just an hour from my home offers one-day opportunities for people like me to "come apart" to spend time with the Lord. If I don't regularly come apart, I will come apart.

It is necessary to get alone with God. Away from the phone, the never-ending household responsibilities, the noise of the radio, television, and computer. To pray. Read Scripture. Journal. Listen. Mostly listen. I set a goal and move toward it. If the Lord has a course adjustment in my settings, it's far easier to steer the direction of a flying plane than one that is parked with the engine turned off.

When guilt holds me back, I can pour out my regrets to the Lord. Accept his forgiveness. If there is sin you or I need to turn away from, then by all means quit. Now. Guilt from the Lord is guilt unto life as a result of legitimate sin. Repent, accept Christ's gift of forgiveness, and move on. Guilt that is not a result of sin is false guilt. It is a burden that serves only to cripple. An excuse. A sign that I am not taking personal responsibility.

We can gently and honestly take stock of ourselves. Give up comparing ourselves to others. God is head over heels, crazy in love with you and me. God is not standing there, hands on hips, hollering, "Come on. You can do better than that. Try harder." No. He stands with his arms outstretched, encouraging us to run into his inviting and accepting embrace.

 I do not try to dance better than anyone else. I only try to dance better than myself.

Mikhail Baryshnikov

"Take my yoke upon you and learn from me, for I am gentle and humble in heart, and you will find rest for your souls. For my yoke is easy and my burden is light" (Matt. 11:29–30).

Looking Glass: You reflect personal responsibility when you take responsibility for your emotions. No one makes you feel a certain way any more than you can control how another feels and reacts. You choose your emotions and behavior. Are you being responsible for your emotions? For your behavior? Or do you allow your emotions and behavior to control you?

 All the art of living lies in a fine mingling of letting go and holding on.

Henry Ellis

◁ Look Back

What is it like to live with you? What habits and characteristics benefit you? What habits and characteristics don't benefit you?

▷ Move Ahead

This week, refuse to blame anyone, including yourself. Each time you are tempted to criticize, condemn, or complain, instead give thanks to God. One friend gave up the three C's from her vocabulary by pay-ing a dollar each time she criticized, condemned, or complained. She put the money toward a charity. It was a win for her and the group she supported.

> One's philosophy is not best expressed in words; it is
> expressed in the choices one makes. In the long run,
> we shape our lives and we shape ourselves. The process
> never ends until we die. And, the choices we make are
> ultimately our own responsibility.
>
> ELEANOR ROOSEVELT

CHAPTER 2

MIRROR, MIRROR

Who am I now that I'm no longer "Mrs."?

What do you call a pocket watch
that is not carried in a pocket?

MY DAUGHTER

Even after he'd been gone for three years, I was blindsided by the fact that I'm a different person single than I was when I was married," my friend described. "I was unprepared for that."

So was I.

Initially, I felt terribly self-conscious. It was awkward sitting by myself even though I'd done it countless times before because he was away on business more often than he was home. But now the empty seat beside me seemed to scream to everyone around, "I'm alone. Not wanted. Not loved. Not cherished. Not valued."

Who am I? Why am I here? And in the dark nights of my soul, I wondered, *What is my significance?*

As a married person, I had roles to play. I covered for his shortcomings, orbited him and his career and desires, and created a family. I was Mrs. So-and-so.

As marrieds, we are viewed by God and society as one flesh. Now I had to adjust to being one whole human being by myself. I had to face my own character flaws that had been camouflaged by the marriage. Or by my status as an abandoned spouse. This experience helped me understand why people remain in toxic relationships.

"I know the marriage is not good," one friend said, "but I decided I would rather tolerate it than be alone. I don't want to be alone."

I was stunned when friends were judgmental and deserted me.

A woman approached me after Sunday school. "I heard you can't make next Saturday's scavenger hunt."

"I'll be out of town."

"It's better that way," she said. "It's for couples anyway and you're alone."

I smiled dumbly and acted like her words didn't hurt. Apparently a team didn't mean partnering with an adult daughter or friend. It meant a spouse. I confess, on vulnerable days such insensitivity persuaded me to shy away from returning to groups such as that class.

Previously, so many visitors included a stay at our house as part of their vacation that I often called our home a bed-and-breakfast. The first year after my husband left, no one came to visit. While others at church talked about the many events on their calendars, my children and I were not invited to any Christmas parties.

The church didn't know what to do with me so they ignored me. Pretended not to see me, didn't ask how I was. The pastor, who agreed separation was necessary, avoided eye contact. Once I telephoned the church office and asked if someone was available to help with a plumbing problem in my bathroom that I didn't know how to tackle. The office said they would get back to me. No one called.

When our soldiers were deployed, the church bent over backward to provide a children's program on Saturdays so the mothers left at home could have a few hours to get to the dentist, doctor, or hairdresser. The church offered teams to rake leaves and do other household maintenance.

I was happy for the help these families received. Their spouses were away for noble reasons. Mine was not. Help offered to military families is short term. Were people afraid that if they helped me once, it would become a long-term obligation?

People distanced themselves from my children. Children's ministry leaders were cool. Families that we had hosted at our home for the holidays for several years suddenly had new plans that did not include us. Another family walked the other way when they saw me at church activities.

The loss of the marriage triggered a never-ending list of losses:

Identity

Spouse

Happily ever after

Stable family relationships

Romance

Plans for a future growing old together, rocking grandbabies on the porch swing

Joyful and peaceful (rather than emotionally charged) pivotal events like graduations, weddings, grandbabies, college visits, and get-togethers with long-distance friends

Honesty between spouses

Honesty between parents and children

Honesty between children

Friendships

The comfort of loving arms

A life partner to assist with decisions and child-raising

Security

A sense of belonging

Income

Medical insurance

Property

Dreams

My history

My marriage certificate was a single page. The divorce document is more than twenty pages. Additional attempts at legal agreements are equally long. The marriage ceremony took six exciting months to plan. The divorce took years of antagonism to hammer out. A spouse who wouldn't honor the marriage certificate isn't likely to honor a protective order or divorce settlement.

Even when the divorce was final, it wasn't over. Without children, I would have quickly relocated and begun a new life, dusting off old dreams, dreaming new ones, and polishing skills and passions I'd shelved when I married.

Yet children bring an eternal connection. Though he was free to go wherever he wanted, the law required I remain within a circumference of my previous spouse. Tethered. Wings clipped. With every telephone call, every weekend visit, every holiday, every child's recital or competition, the heartache is slashed again. Too often a new wound is intentionally inflicted. Divorce didn't make the toxic relationship go away. On my thirtieth wedding anniversary, I sat across the table from my ex while the attorney he hired went for my jugular. I was stunned by the ferocity of hatred that had replaced the covenant to love, honor, and cherish. We'd come a long way, baby, and it was nothing to celebrate.

 Keep your lives free from the love of money and be content with what you have, because God has said, "Never will I leave you; never will I forsake you." So we say with confidence, "The Lord is my helper; I will not be afraid. What can man do to me?"

Hebrews 13:5–6

Alone, I faced myself in the mirror and asked, "Who am I?"
Fearful
Lonely

Hurt
Moody
I'm also . . .
Powerful
Beautiful
Capable
Smart
Creative
Relational
Adventurous
Vivacious
Loving
Expressive
Prosperous
Unforgettable
No longer Mrs., I'm PeggySue.

Four practices helped me begin to focus and develop the authentic me.

1. Practice quiet.

Quiet was necessary for me to hear my own internal voice. And I needed to hear God. Alone in my room each morning, my routine of getting up and preparing for the day was opportunity to hear the Lord. In the quiet, God was able to whisper inspiration into my ear. In the quiet, free of distractions, I could hear him.

I also set aside time for weekly planning and took those plans before the Lord. Quarterly, I invested several quiet hours at home after the children were in bed or while they were otherwise entertained.

2. Practice study.

Daily time in the Bible and reading books by great thinkers expanded my myopic view. Sitting at the feet of inspirational mentors via their books or books about them proved a positive influence. Stories of others who overcame adversity, who made their lives count, provided encouragement.

"I am an A student but I feel like I'm flunking life," I shared with my friend. I searched for new tools to apply to my life. I enrolled in college courses, attended conferences, and took advantage of tutoring opportunities to teach me the skills I needed to enrich my life and life for my children.

3. Practice relationship.

Crabs. The pot was half full of water. The water was half full of crabs. Succulent crustaceans. A delicacy.

Earlier in the day, we had gone crabbing. On a scenic beach pier, enticing tidbits were placed in a wire trap. The baited trap was lowered by rope from the wooden rail until it disappeared into the salty water below. A couple hours later, the trap was hoisted to the surface. Inside were several crabs of satisfactory size. Crabs whose parents failed to warn them about the price attached to a free meal. Crabs who were gullible.

Now these crabs sat in the bottom of the cooking pot, not moving, perhaps taking in this new environment. Maybe glad that the crowded, bumpy ride in a cooler filled with seawater in the back of the car was over.

On the highest setting, the gas flames sizzled the water droplets off the bottom of the pot and gradually, evenly, warmed the water. The molecules in the water moved faster and faster and the temperature started to rise.

Peering over the side, I watched the crabs begin to move. Slowly at first, and then more vigorously, jostling each other. One in particular seemed to take stock of the situation. Climbing atop the others, this crab threw a claw and caught the edge of the pot.

As he hoisted himself out of the hot water and climbed to the top of the pot, another crab reached up his own claw and grabbed the escaping cousin. The nearly free crab fought to keep his hold on the rim but when a second crab also tugged it back down, the adventurous crab lost his hold on potential freedom.

I watched this drama unfold two more times. Then the heat overcame all the crabs and they ended up steaming on a set table between crocks of drawn butter.

Those crabs depicted some of my relationships. I could look back at people that were envious if I experienced success and others that held me back. As a newly single, my relationships were in flux. One day I bemoaned the fact that my stable base of friends had either disconnected or were obviously uncomfortable getting together. They were still couples and I was the fifth wheel. It didn't bother me but was clearly awkward for them. The result was that they avoided me.

"You are an attractive woman," one gal tossed off when I asked why I was no longer included in invitations. That was insulting. Like I would lower myself to flirt with someone else's partner. I wouldn't do that to myself nor would I do that to my children.

A business associate informed me that he would no longer be doing business with me now that I was single. When the shock of these comments subsided, I realized that couples that considered a single to be a threat were saying volumes more about themselves than about me.

"You have to get new friends," my daughter sagely advised.

Loyal to a fault, this was a stretch for me. Yet there was wisdom in her words. It was another place where I had to let go. I had to let go of those relationships. Stop forcing something to work that no longer functioned.

Cultivating new relationships required traveling in different circles. It meant being bold to enter fresh situations and engage in conversations and activities with new people.

I am deeply grateful for the rich friendships that have ridden the good times and the rugged ones with me. "I'm here to make the journey with you," one priceless friend said. What a gift. These precious loved ones have flexed with me, have honestly told me when I needed to hear a view other than my own, have been patient as I proved I make mistakes and need a Savior, and have celebrated God's grace with me. The key was granting all my relationships the freedom to do what was best for them. Some people chose to remain close. Others needed space. A few reconnected later when they were ready.

4. Practice positive self-talk.

My self-talk revealed buckets about what was going on inside my mind. When I realized I was talking to myself in ways I would never speak to another person, it was time to make a change.

Focusing on my negative attributes and shortcomings, listing the things that had gone wrong and the people who had hurt me did not prove inspiring. Nor did it reflect what God said in his love letter about who I am in his eyes. He spoke truth. I was telling myself lies. Emotional curveballs can still send me reeling into old recordings but it doesn't take long to readjust the patterns. The process gets easier.

If you are feeling beaten down, too weary to make improvements, I recommend you listen to your self-talk. If you are saying things to yourself you would never speak aloud to me, then you are telling yourself lies. People who accomplish their dreams use their self-talk to speak kindly and encouragingly to themselves. List your great characteristics. Really. Right now, write down fifty things you truly love about yourself. Do this before you do anything else, including reading further.

"Let's do greatnesses," my youngest frequently suggests. It is one of her favorite family rituals that I learned from someone else. Going around the room, each of us focuses on one person at a time.

"The greatness I see in you, Lilyanna," I say today, "is that you love deeply."

"Yes, I do," she responds with a self-conscious grin.

"The greatness I see in you," her older sister says, "is you are willing to try new things."

"Yes, I am." She beams.

And so it goes with each of us finding a great characteristic about Lilyanna. Then she states a positive characteristic about herself. "I'm a good swimmer," she acknowledges.

"Yes, you are," we chorus.

Then we move to the next person and begin the process all over again with that one.

It is a lot more enjoyable to spotlight each other's positive points and recognize their beneficial traits than pound on the negative qualities. In the same way, repeat to yourself and to your children God's words of love to you:

> For this reason I kneel before the Father, from whom his whole family in heaven and on earth derives its name. I pray that out of his glorious riches he may strengthen you with power through his Spirit in your inner being, so that Christ may dwell in your hearts through faith. And I pray that you, being rooted and established in love, may have power, together with all the saints, to grasp how wide and long and high and deep is the love of Christ, and to know this love that surpasses knowledge—that you may be filled to the measure of all the fullness of God.
>
> Now to him who is able to do immeasurably more than all we ask or imagine, according to his power that is at work within us, to him be glory in the church and in Christ Jesus throughout all generations, for ever and ever! (Eph. 3:14–21)

As part of my healing journey, I attended a leadership conference. After spending several weeks working and growing together, each person in the group was handed three playing cards. We were instructed to give the heart to the person who had most touched our own heart. The diamond was for the individual who displayed the most personal growth. The spade was for the person who had not played full out, for the one who we knew had far more to offer the world.

I'd like to report that I came home with a handful of hearts and diamonds.

I collected all the spades. No kidding. Every one.

Then I was sent outside to silently journal. For forty-five minutes I stared at those black spades. Couldn't these people notice the improvements I had made? Didn't they recognize how far I had already come?

Returning to the conference where the lights were dimmed and soothing music played, I was reduced to a weeping, snotting pile of emotion when my group leader got on his knees in front of each of us and tenderly washed our feet. He began with me.

Once again in our small group, I confided, "I had trouble with those spades."

They somberly shook their heads. "We could see that," one said. "But we didn't mean it as a criticism."

"We can tell that there is a lot more to you," spoke up another.

"The spades are our invitation," said the group leader.

I was confused. "Invitation? What kind of invitation is a spade?"

He leaned forward. "We want you, PeggySue. The real, authentic, genuine, all-out you. All of you."

"You have a beautiful, insightful, tender heart," my teammate said. "But you keep it locked away. We want your heart."

"It's our invitation," said the first group member, "for you to come out and play."

Those of us who have been deeply hurt tend to hold back. We respond by shutting down, buttoning up for fear we may be trampled again. Closed up inside our tight oyster shell, we keep our pearls hidden.

In an attempt to avoid ever feeling the pain of rejection and hurt again, I squashed my ability to feel joy, exuberance, and passion. Emotions are like a bunch of grapes. They are a group. If I numb the negative ones, I also numb the positive ones. If I am going to feel the fun emotions, I must also feel the not so fun ones. It is a package deal. I've since decided that I'd rather take the pain with the joy than not to be whole emotionally. I choose to feel it all, to embrace the entirety rather than robotically feeling nothing.

 To love is to risk not being loved in return. . . . To hope is to risk pain. . . . To try is to risk failure. But risk must be taken because the greatest hazard in life is to risk *nothing*.

Leo Buscaglia

I counted the cost and I would rather risk getting hurt again and live without regrets, fully feeling the love of family and friends and fully giving back love, than continue to hide in that protective, sterile, isolated shell.

God designed for us to play *full out*. The majority plays *not to lose*. Afraid to risk. It is joyful and fulfilling to play to win. He created each of us with a larger-than-life personality. Have a risky kind of day. I invite you, the whole you, the unreserved you, to come out and play.

 The benchmark is you know you've moved on when you can be thankful on some deep level for all the agony.

Mary Coons

◁ Look Back

What major events define your life? What meaning about yourself did you attach to those events?

▷ Move Ahead

Journal or tell about the event from a factual perspective. Leave out the drama, anything that demonstrates a victim mentality. From now on, see the event as a factual incident without adding your perceived meaning. See how this sets you free.

Save the drama
for your mama

T-SHIRT AT THE AIRPORT

CHAPTER 3

BEAUTY AND THE BEAST WITHIN

What am I afraid of?

For God has not given us a spirit of fear,
but of power and of love and of a sound mind.

2 TIMOTHY 1:7 NKJV

Good morning, Lord," is how I would like to greet each day. But when fear dogs my heels, I tightly squeeze my eyes against the intrusion of the sun's early rays until I can no longer deny it is, indeed, morning. On those days, my greeting sounds more like, "Good Lord, it's morning."

What would I do if I weren't afraid? How would I live if I weren't fearful? I made a list:

I wouldn't take garbage from anyone.

I wouldn't accept second best.

I would stop receiving lemons, let alone making lemonade.

I wouldn't be afraid of losing relationships.

I wouldn't be afraid of being left.

I would be financially successful and self-supporting.

I would write freely.

I would . . .

> Be a wildly creative instructor
> Write best-selling screenplays
> Tour countries
> Declutter
> Have fun with my clothing styles
> Organize
> Dance
> Learn to fly
> Complete a college degree
> Love with abandon
> Fall in love
> Believe I am loved
> Believe I am lovable
> Enjoy wealth

Our fears reflect what we most care about, what is most dear to our hearts. At its core, fear is not trusting God. Or myself. Worry is fear in action. It is destructive and suffocating.

Being out of control triggers fear. Yet, when my world appears to be spinning out of check, it is still in God's control. The good news is that I can have liberty from the bondage of worry and anxiety. There will be times when I am frightened, even scared to death, but it doesn't have to paralyze me.

The converse of fear is faith. Faith is a strong belief in who God is. When I walk into a room and see my favorite rocking chair, I have faith that the rocker is constructed to hold me. When I confidently drop my weight into that favorite bentwood, I trust that the chair will keep me from hitting the floor. Faith in God is trusting in his attributes that never change—his grace, compassion, forgiveness, omnipotence, and unconditional love, to name a few. Trust is faith in action.

My reaction to a situation reveals my beliefs far better than the words I say. If I am in a car that is sliding on the ice and I brace myself in anticipation of a collision, that action reflects my beliefs. When the passenger I am with sends up a prayer, "Lord, you are in control, take care of us," that reflects her core beliefs. Same scenario. Two completely different reactions. One reflected faith and trust.

What am I afraid of? I'm fearful of moving ahead with the divorce. Fearful that I will get steamrolled. Fearful that life will be hard. Can I take care of myself? I'm afraid I can't keep deep relationships. I'm fearful of the debt that may be left with me. At a deeper level I wonder, will I be loved? All this makes me not want to get out of bed in the morning. I'm dancing with depression that is a strong leader and a lousy partner.

When I loved a man, I gave him everything. I gave my time, heart, body, goals, and dreams. And when giving all of myself didn't work, I read stacks of self-help books and marriage books for ideas on what to become that he might like better since he didn't like me. This behavior resulted in my complete depletion and loss of self. A million times I became a chameleon in the desperate hope that this time I would be what he wanted. I tried being strong, being neat, being responsible, being the activity director, being his encourager, being forgiving, and being frugal. In the end, none of it worked. All these desperate acrobatics were driven by my desperate neediness that is never attractive to friends, co-workers, or romantic involvements.

"I don't know who I am anymore," I confided to a friend.

"Then it will be fun finding out who you are," she comforted. What she didn't say was that it can be a confusing process akin to being dropped into a foreign country without a map or any clue to the language.

Being consumed with pleasing another is idolatry. I gave up my God-given identity, traded it like arcade tokens for cheap imitations. It is a lack of boundaries and an attempt to merge with someone else until there is no line between where I end and he begins. I was looking for a man to be my savior and I tried to be his.

Even as a young girl I dreamed of Prince Charming, marriage, family, and partnering in significant work. I knew one day my prince would see me, realize I was the gorgeous woman he'd been searching for, fall completely and permanently in love, and we'd live happily ever after. No, I had not experienced this type of family in my childhood. The idea must have come from Disney movies and the internal God-given sense that one day even I would be loved.

Of course, traveling with depression and loneliness are their faithful first cousins, fear and anxiety. Can I do this on my own? How can I make so many decisions by myself? What if I make a mistake? My track record isn't particularly sterling. Am I sufficient to give the children stability and security and positive identity? How should I spend the rest of my life? And the granddaddy of questions, did I make a poor choice?

Fear is an unseen, crippling enemy. Fear chokes, paralyzes, suffocates, and hinders me from living full out. It bleeds the quality from life like smoke depletes clean air from a room.

A rest home study revealed that residents in the winter season of their lives would have done two things differently if they could do life over again. First, they would have taken more risks, and second, they would have done more for the Lord. At the heart of their deepest regrets was fear.

 So do not fear, for I am with you; do not be dismayed, for I am your God. I will strengthen you and help you; I will uphold you with my righteous right hand.

Isaiah 41:10

Fears range from trivial to paralyzing. Frights from mice, spiders, and snakes pale before the fear that floods our veins as single mothers when we wake in the middle of the night wondering how we will raise the children alone, pay the bills, and put new shingles on the roof while dodging the hostile behavior of an unkind ex-spouse. Talk about night sweats. This type descends on single moms of all ages.

One dear friend wrestles with chronic debilitating and occasionally life-threatening illness. There is a terror that accompanies the diagnosis of a terminal disease for ourselves or for beloved friends and family. The alarm of things that go bump in the night fades against the panic that grips a mother who sees her child react to the pain of separated parents by choosing a life apart from God.

By definition, anxiety is a tearing apart. We experience varying degrees ranging from feeling anxious about a new situation to panic that triggers physical tremors, cold sweats, and heart palpitations. In addition to making life miserable, prolonged fear can cause ulcers, sleep loss, panic attacks, and weight fluctuation—not a recommended plan.

Someone gave fear this acronym:

> **F**alse
> **E**vidence
> **A**ppearing
> **R**eal

Left unchecked, fear expands. Abnormal, consistent phobias cripple an otherwise productive life. When my friend had agoraphobia, her overwhelming fear of leaving her own home choked the former passion and potential right out of her.

"Do not be afraid," the Lord says 365 times in the Bible. He said it to every group he talked to. He knows that we are afraid and has already provided for it. Fear is very personal. What I am afraid of may be quite different from what you are afraid of. What don't you trust the Lord with?

In a book I co-wrote with Pat Palau titled *What to Do When You're Scared to Death*, we included several action steps for dealing with fear:

1. List the facts. What is the worst that can happen? What are the advantages of this precarious situation?

2. Face the facts. What are your options? Is there someone you can talk with who has walked this journey before you? Is there a support group? Educate yourself on the topic. We are far more fearful of what we don't understand.

3. Go forward. A lot of scary things have to be done anyway. Most of us have to undergo surgery or at least a root canal sometime. Go in spite of your fear.

4. Take baby steps. Establish a plan for change and daily make small steps of progress toward the larger goal. Like Winston Churchill said, "Never, never, never give up." "He who began a good work in you will carry it on to completion until the day of Christ Jesus" (Phil. 1:6).

5. Live by biblical principles. What do you know about God? Read the Bible and put its principles to practice. Love the Lord with all your heart, soul, mind, and strength. The time is never for irksome, unimportant stressing over temporary, valueless to-do busyness lists. The time is now for the important things with family, friends, and the Lord.

6. Know discouragement is temporary. There will be days when it is difficult to put one foot in front of another. My worst nightmare became reality when my husband chose to leave me and my children. A year later those days of deep emotional pain were less frequent. When I have a day like that now, I know it will pass. I have to walk through it because it is part of the healing process.

7. Record Scripture verses and inspirational quotes. In the Bible, search for encouraging verses. There are lots of them. Memorize God's promises. List the helpful acts people do that become the wind under your wings. Write prayer requests and answered prayers. Read these inspirations when you are gloomy. They are like the stones God told the Israelites to pick up from the bottom of the Jordan when God parted the river and the people crossed to the other side on dry land.

8. *Practice gratitude.* Praise the Lord aloud. Sing hymns and spiritual songs. When people ask, highlight the positives in your life.

9. *Avoid triggers.* Sometimes you must avoid people who cause you to fear and worry. Substitute venomous relationships with ones that inspire you to better choices. Populate your inner circle with special chosen companions.

Guard what you allow into your mind and what you receive in your heart. The eyes and ears are the doorways to our mind and heart and we control what we allow to pass through. "I will set before my eyes no vile thing" (Ps. 101:3). "But the wisdom that comes from heaven is first of all pure; then peace-loving, considerate, submissive, full of mercy and good fruit, impartial and sincere" (James 3:17).

10. *When fear steals your peace, stop and pray.* Like the children of Israel waited in the desert for the pillar of fire by night and the cloud by day to lead them, wait upon the Lord to lead and guide you.

11. *Leave the unknown to the One who knows all things.* Don't try to understand all of life's whys. "The secret things belong to the LORD our God, but the things revealed belong to us and to our children forever" (Deut. 29:29). Trust God. Trust yourself. Trust the process.

 Whether you think that you can, or that you can't, you are usually right.

Henry Ford

◁ Look Back

What are you scared to death of? Because of your fear, what circumstances have you been tolerating or passively resisting? How would you live life differently if you weren't afraid?

▷ Move Ahead

Fear and excitement begin at the same root. When you are fearful, choose to trust God and forge ahead by accepting the emotion of excitement rather than giving in to fear.

Courage does not always roar. Sometimes
courage is the quiet voice at the end of the day saying,
"I will try again tomorrow."

MARY ANNE RADMACHER

CHAPTER 4

SLAY THE DRAGON

Who am I afraid of?

There is neither Jew nor Greek, slave nor free, male nor
female, for you are all one in Christ Jesus.
GALATIANS 3:28

Despite the sleeping aid, I woke in the middle of the night. Again. My heart beat fast and my insides churned. For an hour I tossed and turned, trying to relax, trying to return to much needed sleep. Overwhelming fears ran circles around fruitless attempts to practice relaxation-breathing techniques or recite Scripture.

I dreaded the sunrise. How would I cope with the stress that stole my appetite? The suffocating fear, and its first cousin anxiety, that dominated my situation?

The fear of man is the most stressful problem in life because the stakes are disproportionately high. Problems getting along with people result in strained and broken relationships. On a large scale, they lead to war. Most divorces resemble civil war. Our children are decimated by friendly fire. No wonder we tiptoe around volatile people in hopes of keeping peace.

Those who have been betrayed and abused frequently develop a fear of rejection so extreme that they remain in toxic relationships. Marriage partners who are more cell mates than soul mates are driven by their core belief that a bad relationship is better than none at all. They see themselves as not worthy and valueless. This intense fear of abandonment is housed in neediness, in a loss of self from striving to be what they perceive another person wants. Been there, tried that. It doesn't work.

The common thread is that these are social fears revolving around what people might think. Or what we think they think. We hear about marriages busting apart that looked perfect on the outside and we wonder if our future will be the same. We read of wealthy, sexy, talented entertainers whose husband had an affair and we think, "She had everything. What chance do I have for a happily ever after?"

Ignorance can be a daily source of fear for the newly single. Not knowing how to tackle challenging household maintenance issues, how to negotiate medical and insurance necessities, how to approach a difficult person, or what will happen next. As I face a future I'm not sure of, a future I didn't spend years envisioning, I can choose to be excited about the adventure or I can choose fear. It is too easy to choose fear. My fear of man is fed when I've been abandoned by parents and/or husband and I react by fearing that God doesn't love me either.

Standing at the intersection of choice, if I don't choose to trust God and trust myself, if I don't choose excitement, then fear will enlarge until it determines who I am, what I do or don't do, and where I go. Fear is a greedy despot whose desire for power and control is unquenchable. It swallows me until it is my identity. When a fear is deeply rooted, interrupting life and damaging those we love, then it is time to seek help from a godly, trained counselor.

I was even afraid to call a counselor. When the situation became desperate, I took the phone into my closet and closed the door. Choking back sobs, I made an appointment. Reaching out for professional support before fear ever got to that level would have been easier.

Biblically, the fear of man is rooted in cowardice. We call it excessive people pleasing and codependency. We tell our children not to give in to peer pressure while we do it on an adult level. When I am excessively pleasing to another in an attempt to get that person to give me the acceptance I desire, I am acting selfishly. Labeling my behavior people-pleasing, I behave in a particular manner to manipulate a response I need. Rather than relying on the Lord to meet my needs, I am expecting another person to be my savior. All because I perceive another person to be better than me.

When I care more about what others may think than I do about what God thinks, I have placed people above God. "You shall have no other gods before me," the Lord declares in Exodus 20:3.

Codependency and people pleasing are new terms for an old behavior. King Solomon was familiar with this. He said, "Fear of man will prove to be a snare, but whoever trusts in the LORD is kept safe" (Prov. 29:25). A snare is a trap. No one deliberately falls into a trap. Yet being controlled by fear is an enslaving noose.

A snare has a deceiving degree of attractiveness. That is what makes the trap effective. I look at all the benefits I think I will receive if I am in the good graces of a particular person—attention, affection, belonging, companionship, connecting. Maybe status, financial support, romance, an occasional back rub.

What I don't admit is that if I must manipulate these responses through people-pleasing behavior, I will never truly be content for two reasons. First, I'm exhausted from perpetually performing to get what I want. I'm not being authentic to myself or to this other person. Second, the responses I receive are unsatisfying, not freely given, and are not genuine acts of the true love I yearn for. Once tangled in this performance cycle, I am sidetracked from my God-given purpose. This trap entangles me in a sense of helplessness and insecurity. No wonder Solomon called the fear of man a snare.

The fear of man, what others think of us, is somewhere in the equation for most of us who are suddenly single. We fear abandonment, betrayal, loneliness, and rejection. If not addressed, these strong fears hold us in unhealthy relationships and cause women to repeat them.

One woman described, "I allowed my fears to overrule my heart and compromise healthy relationship boundaries. I sacrificed my principles. I gave up college, gave in to sex, and when a pregnancy resulted, I gave in to an abortion. When he wasn't faithful, I tried to be more of this, better at that, always available so he would love me. This noxious cycle perpetuated because I was more concerned about pleasing a man than about pleasing the Lord."

Ironically, despite all my efforts to please a man with my performance, my marriage died. Exhausted, I wanted to blame everything on him. But the harsh truth is that the fear of man is self-centered. It's all about me. It is impossible to focus on my fear, and how I am going to get through or around it, and at the same time demonstrate a healthy interest in the well-being of others.

The solution to the fear of man is simple. "Do not be afraid of those who kill the body but cannot kill the soul. Rather, be afraid of the One who can destroy both soul and body in hell" (Matt. 10:28). The solution to the fear of man is to play to an audience of One. The rest falls into place.

Playing to an audience of One is to be genuine and authentic to myself and concerned only about being in relationship with God. He promised that his yoke is easy and his burden is light. When I'm stressed, tense, and performing like a hamster on a wheel, I've stepped out of the easy comfort of relationship with the Lord and I've returned to striving to get my needs met through people pleasing.

 You gain strength, courage, and confidence by every experience in which you really stop to look fear in the face. You are able to say to yourself, "I lived through this horror. I can take the next thing that comes along." You must do the thing you think you cannot do.

Eleanor Roosevelt

◁ Look Back

Recall your most embarrassing moment. Who were you trying to please or impress in that instance? Who is it that you care deeply what they think of you? Do these concerns about people and organizations supersede your concern for what God thinks?

▷ Move Ahead

One day at a time, practice playing only to an audience of One. Grant yourself the freedom to be genuine to yourself, to others, and to God.

Let the past sleep, but let it sleep on the bosom of Christ, and go out into the irresistible future with him.

OSWALD CHAMBERS

CHAPTER 5

Knight in Shining Armor

Does Prince Charming exist?

All human beings have two things in common; we all
experience pain, and we all need a Savior.

PEGGYSUE WELLS

How do you receive love?"

I was allotted forty-five minutes to journal around the question. The assignment seemed easy enough. Until I got outside and all alone with myself, my heart, and my blank notebook. I'm a writer, for Pete's sake. I've written books, curriculum, screenplays, letters, and thousands of articles. Filling a piece of paper doesn't even make me break a sweat.

Until today.

Until this question.

I didn't have an answer.

As I searched for something to write, I crashed into memories of sabotaged dreams, patterns of sacrificed passions, feelings of inconveniencing others when I had a birthday or a gift I wanted for Christmas. Unworthiness. I hadn't been loved by a significant person in my life and I had allowed that to color everything else.

The better part of an hour was spent in anger and frustration, silently raging and cursing as that blank piece of paper accused me of not allowing myself to receive love. True, someone whose love I needed had withheld it. Someone who had vowed to love, honor, and cherish me until death did us part. But that sheet of paper revealed to me that I had attached a meaning to the choices my spouse had made. The fact was he didn't love me. Using that fact as proof, I had judged myself not worthy of love and had stopped receiving it from any other sources.

I could have been the visual aid for the Scarlett O'Hara syndrome. In the classic film *Gone With the Wind*, stunning and self-centered Scarlett was so consumed with the one thing she didn't have—her best friend's husband—that she never saw what she did have. She never saw that she had a beautiful home, a lovely daughter, and Clark Gable as the roguish husband who loved her.

All I saw was the lack. What I didn't see, indescribably larger than the subject of my narrow-minded view, was my glorious Heavenly Bridegroom. Eclipsing my loss, the Lord offered joy and abundance. He cherished me and delighted in showering me with the delights of my heart. Long before I was even born, he loved me with an everlasting love that was pure. No strings attached. No performance necessary.

> On the day you were born your cord was not cut, nor were you washed with water to make you clean, nor were you rubbed with salt or wrapped in cloths. No one looked on you with pity or had compassion enough to do any of these things for you. Rather, you were thrown out into the open field, for on the day you were born you were despised.
>
> Then I passed by and saw you kicking about in your blood, and as you lay there in your blood I said to you, "Live!" I made you grow like a plant of the field. You grew up and developed and became the most beautiful of jewels. Your breasts were formed and your hair grew, you who were naked and bare.

Later I passed by, and when I looked at you and saw that you were old enough for love, I spread the corner of my garment over you and covered your nakedness. I gave you my solemn oath and entered into a covenant with you, declares the Sovereign Lord, and you became mine. (Ezek. 16:4–8)

It's not the miracle I've prayed for. When a little girl was told that the Lord was always with her, she replied, "Can I have someone with skin on?" I wanted a human prince charming. Like an old *Star Trek* episode, my prayer is more like Captain Kirk's communication to Scotty, "Beam me out of here." Sometimes it sounds like, "Beam me up, Scotty. There's no intelligent life here."

Occasionally God does just that. He rescues me from the sticky problem or removes the sticky wicket from me. But far more frequently the Lord comes to be with me in the storm in the same way he came walking on the Sea of Galilee to be with the disciples when their boat was caught in a raging tempest.

 He heals the brokenhearted and binds up their wounds.

Psalm 147:3

When Shadrach, Meshach, and Abednego wouldn't worship King Nebuchadnezzar's statue, these Hebrew-captives-turned-king's-staff were threatened with capital punishment.

"O Nebuchadnezzar," they said, "we do not need to defend ourselves before you in this matter. If we are thrown into the blazing furnace, the God we serve is able to save us from it, and he will rescue us from your hand, O king. But even if he does not, we want you to know, O king, that we will not serve your gods or worship the image of gold you have set up" (Dan. 3:16–18).

If I were in their sandals, I would have been begging Scotty to beam me out of that situation.

Pressured to compromise their faith, these men wouldn't bend or bow. They'd rather burn. Just for them, the king had the fire stoked ten times hotter. "The king's command was so urgent and the furnace so hot that the flames of the fire killed the soldiers who took up Shadrach, Meshach and Abednego, and these three men, firmly tied, fell into the blazing furnace" (Dan. 3:22–23).

Though I'm certain the three accused men prayed fervently that they would not have to encounter the furnace, the Lord did not deliver them from their sentence. Instead, they miraculously not only didn't burn but the Lord met them inside the flames. King Nebby declared, "Look! I see four men walking around in the fire, unbound and unharmed, and the fourth looks like a son of the gods" (Dan. 3:25).

God was with the three in the fiery furnace. The only thing that burned was the rope that bound them.

"It couldn't have been all bad," my friend said after I once again whined about how I was a victim of my circumstances.

Initially I was angry at the callous comment. Obviously my friend was not shoveling out the sympathy I was seeking. The comment also haunted me. I began to look at my fiery furnace differently. My resentment about going into the situation had blocked me from seeing who was there with me.

What fire are you going through? Look closely and you will notice that the Lord is with you. Quietly perhaps. He is a gentleman after all. But he is there. When I embarked on a God hunt searching for the Lord's fingerprints in my days instead of focusing on the problems and loss, I found he was right there and far more involved than I realized. He doesn't always rescue us out of our circumstances but he does promise to walk with us through them.

My Heavenly Bridegroom was, and is, faithfully in love with me always. In Jane Austen's classic tale, *Sense and Sensibility*, the noble Colonel Christopher Brandon is head over heels in love with the young and spritely Marianne Dashwood, who is too naive to understand the maturity and depth of her admirer. Colonel Brandon selflessly guards Marianne's heart at every opportunity while honoring her freedom to make her choices. Watching Colonel Brandon's emotional agony as he longs to fully love Marianne and have her love him in return, I long for my own Colonel Brandon.

Sitting behind me in the movie theater is the Lord who selflessly guards my heart at every opportunity while honoring my freedom to make my choices. He longs to fully love me and have me love him in return.

In Jane Austen's *Pride and Prejudice*, Mr. Darcy selflessly and discreetly invests his time and money to benefit the opinionated Elizabeth Bennet. Because he cares deeply for Elizabeth, those who are valuable to Elizabeth, including her family—both good and foolish—have value to Mr. Darcy. Elizabeth's admirer's affections are demonstrated by his consistent, gentle guarding of her heart and well-being, without any strings attached. Mr. Darcy did not demand that Elizabeth repay his kindness, nor did he even make known his efforts on her behalf.

The Lord is a lover of even deeper quality than Colonel Brandon or Mr. Darcy. And best of all, unlike the fictional heroes of Jane Austen's literature (who are patterned after Christ), the Lord and his great love is real! An author himself, the Lord gave several illustrations of his love to help me understand the maturity and depth of my lover. In the book of Ruth, Boaz is a picture of my Heavenly Bridegroom. Boaz protected Ruth physically, emotionally, and spiritually. He protected her reputation, her innocence, and her purity. He provided for her and her mother-in-law. He was kind, gentle, and strong for her.

In the same way, my Heavenly Bridegroom is kind, gentle, and strong for me. He provides forgiveness and salvation for me that I cannot achieve for myself. He promised to never leave me nor forsake me. He has secured eternity for me, is preparing a splendid place for me in Heaven, and promised to return for me so we can spend eternity together.

Some of us desire Prince Charming to arrive on his great charger and rescue us from our pain, circumstances, and the drudgery of life.

Prince Charming already arrived. It's time to get dressed for the ball, Cinderella!

The Lord is the quintessential Prince Charming. He is the archetype, the ideal of what every woman's heart longs for. This hero loves with all his heart, wrote a timeless love letter, loves unconditionally, provides and protects, enCOURAGEs me to pursue my dreams and passions, listens without interrupting, is with me always, is stronger than the bad guys, treats me with honor and respect, and cares about what is important to me. He cherishes me.

 You have made known to me the path of life; you will fill me with joy in your presence, with eternal pleasures at your right hand.

Psalm 16:11

Historically, our Heavenly Bridegroom fights on our behalf against principalities and dark evils. When my disobedience to God separated me from heaven and damned me to eternity in hell, Christ sacrificed himself, gave his life for mine on the cross to provide forgiveness, salvation, reconciliation, and eternal relationship. It was his free gift. No strings attached.

Like the grand knight that saves the beautiful princess, at the end of time astride a white charger this compassionate warrior will face my archenemy, the dragon, in a vast conflagration. He will battle the enemy of my soul, sending the author of evil and the malevolent beast into the everlasting abyss.

As King of kings, my Heavenly Bridegroom offers me royalty in an eternal kingdom. Even when I have not been in relationship with him, the Lord discreetly and selflessly invested himself to provide for and to protect me. To love me. Without demands and never bullying or controlling, he is our ultimate true lover.

My love story with my Heavenly Bridegroom has all the components of the best romance tale, the ultimate chick flick. It stars a great heroine (me! and you!), and it features true romance as the hero woos us, a really bad guy, and a just and satisfying ending. In the midst of danger, jeopardy, and poor choices, my noble lover is concerned to protect his beloved physically, emotionally, and spiritually. Seeing in me what no one else notices, he is mindful of my purity, my reputation, and those who are dear to me. The best part of this adventure romance is that it's true. The best part of this Prince Charming is that far from fiction, imagination, makeup, costumes, special effects, and contrived screen idols, he is real.

 Love is patient, love is kind. It does not envy, it does not boast, it is not proud. It is not rude, it is not self-seeking, it is not easily angered, it keeps no record of wrongs. Love does not delight in evil but rejoices with the truth. It always protects, always trusts, always hopes, always perseveres. Love never fails.

1 Corinthians 13:4–8

Someone once advised that a woman is happiest in a marriage where the groom loves the bride more than the bride loves the groom. That is certainly the case in our relationship with our Heavenly Bridegroom. We can't out-give or out-love this Heavenly Incurable Romantic. Knowing this, why don't we all run, dash, sprint, race, careen, and fly with arms outstretched into the loving embrace of our Heavenly Bridegroom?

The key to receiving love is to accept the Lord's love. Can you and I define ourselves as radically beloved by God? This is our true self. Every other identity is an illusion. No matter how I feel, the cross proves that I am loved.

Can I trust myself to recognize love? What I thought was romantic love was a delusion of my own creation. But I have learned a few things since then. Mistakes are valuable experiences when we learn from them.

Can I receive God's love into my life? This is the first and healthiest step to receiving love and being able to love.

◁ Look Back

How do you refuse love? How do you receive love?

▷ Move Ahead

Daily read a chapter in Scripture, highlighting passages where God speaks of his love. Each week, do something special for yourself. Honor yourself. Treat yourself as well as you treat a guest or a date.

I have loved you with an everlasting love; I have drawn
you with loving-kindness.

JEREMIAH 31:3

CHAPTER 6

READ THE STORY

Is there a love story for me?

Life does not cease to be funny when people die any
more than it ceases to be serious when people laugh.

GEORGE BERNARD SHAW

Having trouble mustering up thankfulness? Does joy sound as far away as a vacation on Venus?

"The pain in my heart is so intense it feels like a physical pain," I confided. "I'm desolately lonely. I'm without vision or future. The children need a strong, capable mom. They also cross and challenge me. I'm beat down, weary, rejected."

It was at my daughter's Christmas concert while the choir sang about the wonders of Christ's birth that I realized I believed the promises of the Bible—for everyone but me. Pressed down and depressed, I resembled a stray cat staring through a window at all the happy chosen people inside. I felt that God had abandoned and neglected me.

Since that isn't how a good parent treats a child, I surmised that I was not one of God's chosen. God didn't want me either. I had tried.

I had given my all to make my marriage work. Dishonored and disgraced, I was bitter at my failure and disappointed with God who hadn't helped me fix it. Who didn't do it my way.

But like Peter when Jesus asked, "You do not want to leave, too, do you?" I realized there is nowhere else to go. "Simon Peter answered him, 'Lord, to whom shall we go? You have the words of eternal life. We believe and know that you are the Holy One of God'" (John 6:67–69). Like David, I echoed, "I would rather be a doorkeeper [or a stray cat] in the house of my God than dwell in the tents of the wicked" (Ps. 84:10).

When your world is turned upside down, the quickest way to gather some semblance of sanity is to press into the Lord. Like David, I can say that my prayers often felt like they were bouncing off brass skies. Yet, though sometimes quiet, the Lord is the one constant in a very inconsistent world. Devotions is where we begin.

Why? What's the point of investing seven, fifteen, or thirty minutes regularly in this activity, especially when you and I are exhausted, overwhelmed, and have a thousand other responsibilities demanding our time?

It's about eternal life. For me. For you. For our children. Today it may feel like you're trapped in a war zone. But eternity looms ahead and it's . . . well, it's eternal. Life is like living on a battle ship. Jesus Christ called us to occupy until his return. When this is all over, I'm signed up for the eternal luxury cruise.

It's about having an anchor when the storms of life are swamping my boat. It's about having a compass through the desert of dailyness. It's about finding rest in the oasis of the love letter God composed to you and me.

When there is an enormous hole in my heart, a chasm in my dreams, it is important to make wise choices about how I'm going to medicate that pain. Where will I turn to fill that void?

There are wholesome (pun intended) responses I can choose. Instinct drives too many of us to ridiculous actions ranging from rushing into a second-rate replacement relationship to numbing our-selves with alcohol, drugs, spending, or sleep. The one response I will not regret is to run into the embrace of the Lord. "And the peace of God, which transcends all understanding, will guard your hearts and your minds in Christ Jesus" (Phil. 4:7).

There is a world of difference between a performance-based man-ner of earning God's approval and having a relationship with the Lord. I can be a Martha who does tasks or I can be a Mary who sits with Jesus and soaks in his presence.

When my daughter visits, I can spend hours cleaning the house and preparing her favorite dishes, or I can sit with her over tea and take-out Chinese food relishing every moment of conversation and opportunity to be with her. The first option demonstrates love through works. Yet, the second option is superior because it is the gift of presence. It is relationship at a deeper level.

I can know a lot about a famous person or a historical person-ality without knowing that person. I've written biographies about Grammy Award–winning musicians so I can tell you a good deal about each individual, about his or her life and journey to stardom. But I do not know that musician personally. We don't get together for lunch, e-mail our hellos, or exchange Christmas cards. While I know a lot about them, it is doubtful that the objects of my research know I exist.

On the other hand, I have a close friend who I talk with regularly and we have a history together. I know what piece of jewelry wound up in her vacuum cleaner, and she knows how I came to own a pet goose. We share a love for books, deep discussions, chocolate chip scones, and tea. I talk more than she does and she is wiser. In addition to knowing *about* each other, we *know* each other.

How do you and I choose to be with our Lord? How do we develop a deeper relationship with our Heavenly Bridegroom?

Reading the Bible is a source of comfort and a never ending well of fresh discoveries. In a journal I jot down thoughts, insights, questions, and favorite phrases. Don't allow much time to pass without reading God's love letter to you. Stuart Briscoe advises our head never hit the pillow without first being in the Word.

 The Word of the Lord is a light to guide you, a counselor to counsel you, a staff to support you, a sword to defend you, and a physician to cure you.

Thomas Brooks

How should we approach the Bible? Look up a key word in the concordance at the back of the Bible to find various verses on a topic? Follow a reading guide that takes us systematically through the whole Bible?

In our book *What to Do When You're Scared to Death*, my friend and co-author Pat Palau described, "The God who knows you and me inside and out is aware of our needs and can speak to us through the process of spending time in the Word." In other words, it doesn't matter what method we use. "Sometimes I cannot articulate a specific verse that answers my specific problem," Pat said. "I read the passage for the day, and sensed that God had spoken, 'Whether you turn to the right or to the left, your ears will hear a voice behind you, saying, "This is the way; walk in it"' (Isa. 30:21). He was there with me, and would see me through. I felt my scattered, wild thoughts come under the control of the Holy Spirit, calming me down."[1]

I read Scripture with two questions. Is God worthy of my trust and my heart? Does God love me?

In Central America, I worked with a team among the poor, giving medical care to over three hundred patients, mostly women and children. We took temperatures and blood pressures, bathed infected feet, distributed doctor-prescribed medications, and shampooed countless heads of lice. Through broken Spanish, a couple brilliant interpreters, smiles, hugs, and gestures, we communicated and connected.

One day our group was invited for an extended visit at a potter's home. The artisan demonstrated how he intimately works with the clay he mines from the ground, mixes with water and river sand, and shapes on his wheel. His hands tenderly cupped around the form-ing vessel, he gently removes impurities and carefully adds his unique design and finish. Then the exquisite piece emerges from the fire as a one-of-a-kind collector's item. Just like you. Just like me.

As we traveled, always in the background was the low cloud of smoke that marked the location of the dump. For generations, people have lived at this seemingly uninhabitable place, scratching out an existence by reselling what they scrounge from the foul-smelling rubbish heaps. Mothers have been known to give their daughters to drivers in exchange for first pick of the trash collec-tion truck. One missionary befriended a family from the dump, built them a home in a better neighborhood, and moved them to the new location. Yet money, education, and improved politics did not cure their poverty. Six months later the family had returned to the dump.

Women from teens to *abuelas* (grandmothers) attended a two-day conference. From my heart I spoke about my insecurity around being chosen and loved by God. For a long time I had viewed my relation-ship with the Lord through my worst experiences with people while Scripture urged me to see myself through God's loving eyes. Though from another country, a different culture, and a different language, tears flowed as these women expressed similar doubts regarding their relationship with the Lord. Was God worthy of their trust and heart? Did he love them?

Jesus died for my sins and conquered death to give me forgiveness and eternal life with him, and God provided his written word for me in the form of the Bible. In effect, God compassionately moved me out of the dump. For me to shrug all that off—to point to one or three people who hurt me and say that proves I am not lovable—is the equivalent of hunching my shoulders against God's heartfelt gift and slinking back to cough among the trash and perpetual smoke of the toxic landfill.

"Have you forgiven those who hurt you?" It was a great question from my daughter.

"Some days, yes," I answered. "Other days, new hurts are inflicted."

"Instead of approaching every situation from the assumption you are unlovable and abandoned, and collecting evidence to prove you are right, why not approach every situation from God's viewpoint that you are cherished? Find evidence to prove God right."

Based on results, what I had been doing wasn't working. Time for something different. I embraced her challenge, journaled daily evidence of God's love and highlighted his declarations of devotion in the Bible.

I've never gone back. Never returned to dump thinking. I comb through God's word, seeking, trusting, and believing the great things he says about me. It is a joyful, freeing, powerful experience to accept and believe God's written Word, the Bible. To know I am not the stray cat, but his beautiful and cherished bride.

"The LORD appeared to us in the past, saying: 'I have loved you with an everlasting love; I have drawn you with loving-kindness.'" (Jer. 31:3)

"The LORD your God is with you, he is mighty to save. He will take great delight in you, he will quiet you with his love, he will rejoice over you with singing." (Zeph. 3:17)

"Your love, O LORD, reaches to the heavens, your faithfulness to the skies. Your righteousness is like the mighty mountains, your justice like the great deep. O LORD, you preserve both man and beast. How priceless is your unfailing love! Both high and low among men find refuge in the shadow of your wings. They feast on the abundance of your house; you give them drink from your river of delights. For with you is the fountain of life; in your light we see light." (Ps. 36:5–9)

"Never will I leave you; never will I forsake you." (Heb. 13:5)

The words of love and heartening promises are there as proof that the Lord is worthy to be trusted. He is worthy of, and will nobly protect, the rare and priceless treasure of a woman's heart. He provided the Bible to remind you and me, over and over again, day after day, that he loves us. And as he communicates his love to me, then I respond with declarations of my own love for him. Our relationship naturally transitions from his one-sided wooing of me, his bride, to a fulfilling two-sided, interactive love story.

I begin and end my day with prayer. It is the first thing I breathe when I wake up. Connecting with the Lord sets the context for the day. I am never alone. And I rely on the Lord's guidance. Prayer is my last thought as I fall asleep. There is a comfort to slip into slumber in the protective presence of God.

Prayer is simply talking to God like we talk to our best friend. The way we talk to our true life's partner. Honest. Authentic. Real.

Then listen. I like to be quiet and allow God to speak back to my heart and spirit. I tell God my concerns. Okay, sometimes I blatantly, unequivocally whine. I ask or even beg for help with challenges. I also thank him for the good things.

Like any relationship, conversation with the Lord does best when it is regular and undistracted. I knit into the routine consistent triggers for prayer. First thing in the morning while I dress is a perfect opportunity to leave off the radio. In the stillness, I anchor my day and my thoughts in conversation with the Lord. In the hush, I hear him when he inspires me with fresh ideas and insights, and new mechanisms to approach challenges.

The children and I thank the Lord for our meals, of course, and there are many other regular opportunities for connecting. Driving lends itself to prayer. We pray each time we get in the car. When I am alone in the car, I spend quiet time with the Lord, bringing my wildly scattered thoughts that ricochet like a ball in a pinball machine into the peace and centeredness of the Lord. When I am not alone in the car, we are confined in a small space for a time and can pray together.

I enjoy praying God's grace and blessing over my children when they go to sleep. I also do this with visitors as they leave. When someone shares a concern, I pray for them right at that moment, whether we are together or over the phone. Like the priests who brought the twelve tribes of Israel before the Lord's remembrance, represented by colored stones on their breastplate, it is an honor to bring others to the Lord. Like the four friends did for the paralyzed man on his mat, we occasionally carry someone onto the roof and lower them into the Lord's presence. When talking to God is a habit, I am like those four friends in the Bible story. I know where to find the Lord and I am confident about what he can do.

Prayer is talking to the Lord about myself, my concerns, and about those I care about. It is bringing before the throne those who desire to know that God cares for them.

◁ Look Back

What are your feelings toward the Lord? You can be honest because the Lord knows your heart already. He is big enough to handle it, and he'll help you deal with any anger or mistrust between you.

▷ Move Ahead

Throughout the Bible, God tells us about himself and invites us to know and be connected with him. Keep a journal where you record evidence that proves you are loved and that God is trustworthy and faithful. Include Scripture as well as those day-to-day God sightings that remind you he is head over heels in love with you.

When you pass through the waters,
I will be with you;
and when you pass through the rivers,
they will not sweep over you.
When you walk through the fire,
you will not be burned;
the flames will not set you ablaze.

ISAIAH 43:2

CHAPTER 7

SHARE THE STORY

How do I share that love story with my children?

Hear, O Israel: The LORD our God, the LORD is one. Love
the LORD your God with all your heart and with all your
soul and with all your strength. These commandments
that I give you today are to be upon your hearts.
Impress them on your children. Talk about them when
you sit at home and when you walk along the road,
when you lie down and when you get up.

DEUTERONOMY 6:4–7

My friend Char calls me the great connector. She knows I am passionate about introducing people with common interests. Then I get to watch as the chemistry of like-minded people propels them forward to easily do in concert what they struggled to do alone. What glory to be the one who introduces my child to Jesus Christ.

"Jesus answered, 'I am the way and the truth and the life. No one comes to the Father except through me'" (John 14:6).

"The LORD is my shepherd; I shall not want" (Ps. 23:1 NKJV).

"For there is one God and one mediator between God and men,

the man Christ Jesus, who gave himself as a ransom for all men" (1 Tim. 2:5–6).

"But as many as received Him, to them He gave the right to become children of God" (John 1:12 NKJV).

"Every good and perfect gift is from above, coming down from the Father of the heavenly lights, who does not change like shifting shadows" (James 1:17).

Family devotions are designed to make the children and me familiar with God's instructions for life—the Bible. From 2 Timothy 3:16–17 we learn that "all Scripture is God-breathed and is useful for teaching, rebuking, correcting and training in righteousness, so that the man of God may be thoroughly equipped for every good work."

I tutor my children in school subjects including reading, math, science, and history. I teach them socially acceptable behaviors including to floss their teeth, wash behind their ears, keep their finger out of their nostrils or anyone else's, drink water, and eat fruits and vegetables so they don't get scurvy. When they are older I remind them to rotate their tires and balance their finances. Certainly I want to include tutoring them in spiritual matters.

I want my nearest and dearest to know that Scripture says, "Anyone who trusts in him will never be put to shame" (Rom. 10:11).

When they wonder if they are special, I want to have shared with them that God said, "For there is no difference between Jew and Gentile—the same Lord is Lord of all and richly blesses all who call on him, for, 'Everyone who calls on the name of the Lord will be saved'" (Rom. 10:12–13).

Scripture asks, "How, then, can they call on the one they have not believed in? And how can they believe in the one of whom they have not heard?" (Rom. 10:14). How indeed, if I have not told them?

As parents we research lots of educational options for our youngsters. Educating my children about the Lord is not to be missed. Proverbs 1:7 states, "The fear of the LORD is the beginning of knowledge."

Affectionately called "Bible time" at our home, family devotions are simple. Bible time is, first and foremost, reading the Bible.

Reading Scripture

We began by reading one chapter aloud followed by prayer. While we started with a good children's Bible when the children were young, we transitioned into a real Bible as soon as possible. My favorite versions are the Geneva Bible for study notes and the New International Version for easy reading. We took turns reading so each person became comfortable reading Scripture.

For those new to the idea, start with the book of Esther. This story has all the elements of an adventure movie. A beautiful girl with a mysterious identity, a powerful king seeking a bride, a cunning enemy with a seemingly foolproof plot to kill the queen and her people, a brave relative, and a clever twist of events which conclude in a satisfying ending. This is great stuff. Who said the Bible is boring?

The book of Ruth is another good introduction to the sixty-six books of the Bible. Ruth is a refreshing look at true love. Ruth found herself going it alone after her husband died. In fact, there are three women in this story who found themselves without a life partner.

My favorite part about the book of Ruth is the comforting picture it presents of Jesus, the forever lover of our soul. Using Boaz as a depiction, the story assures us that the Lord is concerned about our heart, is protective of you and me, provides for us, and looks out for our good reputation. Not a Bozo, Boaz reminds us how a woman is supposed to be honored by a man. Ruth and Boaz had a son who became the grandfather of King David, the great-something grandfather of the Messiah. It doesn't get better.

Of course, girls are intrigued by the commoner-turned-princess in Esther, and the true love found by Ruth, while boys are fascinated with noble Boaz, King David's mighty men, Daniel's brave encounter with the lions, and Joseph's rise to power in Egypt.

Once we were in the habit of reading aloud a chapter of the Bible each day, we added a Psalm. These poetic writings led us to worship. Proverbs was the next good addition. There are thirty-one chapters in Proverbs, one for each day of the month. Coincidence? Convenient. These little beauties are packed with wisdom for successful living and loving.

Eventually we were reading one chapter from the Old Testament, one from Psalms, the Proverb of the day, and a chapter from the New Testament.

The simple read-aloud time frequently generated questions that led to lively discussions and stimulated additional research. The children posed some of their questions to the pastor.

Memorizing

We memorized the books of the Bible first, so we would become familiar with the what and where of the Bible. We recited the first five books three times in a row each day. When those flowed easily, we added the next five to the singsong we made up. Before long, all sixty-six books were committed to memory. To celebrate, each one who recited the books of the Bible was given a Bible of their own.

Favorite verses, passages, and chapters we memorized together, one verse at a time. Our favorite version for memorization is the New King James Version. The poetic wording is beautiful and easy to commit to memory.

 Your word I have hidden in my heart, that I might not sin against You.

Psalm 119:11 NKJV

During Bible time, we repeat a verse three times. When that verse is memorized, we add the next and say that one three times. There is no time pressure. Memorizing John 3:16 may take a week. It may take two.

When we had several passages memorized such as the Ten Commandments, John 1:1–14, and the Lord's Prayer, we rehearsed each memorized portion once a week. This came after we spent several months memorizing the Ten Commandments one verse at a time, patted ourselves on the back for accomplishing this, and promptly forgot it.

Favorite Scriptures to memorize include:

+ John 3:16
+ John 1:1–14
+ Exodus 20:1–17
+ 1 Corinthians 13
+ 2 Timothy 1:7
+ Matthew 6:9–13
+ Psalm 23
+ Psalm 100

We added the Christmas story (Luke 2:1–20 and Matt. 2:1–15), the Easter story, and individual verses. When my children outgrew my continual oversight and were choosing their own reading material, films, and entertainment, I equipped them with a litmus test by which to select their media: we memorized Philippians 4:8, "Finally, brothers, whatever is true, whatever is noble, whatever is right, whatever is pure, whatever is lovely, whatever is admirable—if anything is excellent or praiseworthy—think about such things."

Here's an example of our Scripture memory review schedule:

Monday	Deuteronomy 6:4–9; The Lord's Prayer (Matt. 6:9–13)
Tuesday	10 Commandments (Ex. 20:3–17); John 1:1–14
Wednesday	Books of the Bible; Psalm 100
Thursday	Christmas Story (Luke 2:1–20, Matt. 2:1–15)
Friday	1 Corinthians 13; Psalm 23

Singing

Sometimes we sing. The younger children particularly enjoy fast numbers with movements. For me, it is hard to sing when I'm in emotional pain but once I begin, even through gritted teeth, a lot of the weight of the world drops off my shoulders like a soldier shedding his seventy-pound rucksack. Initially reluctant, teens relax into the music and even get into the cheesy movements with younger siblings before shifting into favorite praise songs.

Praying

We always close by praying aloud together, beginning with the youngest and ending with the oldest, which is typically me. When the youngest asks to go backward, I get to go first. To help her children become comfortable with prayer, my friend encouraged her young ones to tell God one grumbly thing and one good thing.

One of my children started a notebook where we recorded prayer requests, answered prayers, and things we were thankful for. It was a boost for our faith to look back on what God had done on our behalf.

 Call to me and I will answer you and tell you great and unsearchable things you do not know.
Jeremiah 33:3

Similarly, one friend highlights the verses the family memorizes in the Bible and writes answered prayers and noteworthy remembrances along the margins. Their family Bible is a family history of God's interactions with their household.

Blessing

Last, I added a blessing, something we saw modeled in Scripture. Over and over the patriarchs spoke a blessing over their children. As I read through the Bible, each time I came across uplifting words of grace, I added them to my list of blessings to say over my children. In between, my standard blessing quickly became, "The LORD bless you and keep you; the LORD make His face shine upon you, and be gracious to you; the LORD lift up His countenance upon you, and give you peace" (Num. 6:24–26 NKJV).

Whether we gather for family devotions in the morning, after dinner, or at bedtime, blessing the children with verses from Scripture is a reassuring way to send everyone off to the next thing on the agenda.

My favorite blessings to say over my children are:

+ Numbers 6:24–26
+ Ephesians 3:14–21

Other options include:

+ Genesis 12:2–3
+ Deuteronomy 28:3–6
+ Psalm 20
+ Romans 15:5–6, 13
+ 2 Thessalonians 2:16–17
+ Hebrews 13:20–22
+ Jude 1:24–25

This is what worked at my house. You can cannibalize the good ideas that fit for your family and discard the rest, or save it for another time when it does apply. Anyone who says there is a right or wrong way to do devotions needs medication for legalism. The important thing was for us to find an easy method that regularly got us into the Bible and into relationship with the Lord. It is a forever foundation of truth we can lean on when so much has proven unfaithful.

To sum it up, start with first things first. Begin reading a chapter in the Bible each day and pray aloud together. That's enough. As you are ready, expand the reading to include a chapter from the Old Testament, one from the New Testament, one from Psalms, and one from Proverbs. One by one, add in the other components. If you want to.

Our family devotional time looks something like this:

1. Read one chapter in children's picture Bible and/or one chapter in the Old Testament
2. Sing praises
3. Read a psalm

4. Memory review
5. Read one chapter in Proverbs
6. Practice new memory verse
7. Read one chapter in the New Testament
8. Family prayer
9. Blessing

Encouraging Tips

1. Don't quit if you miss a day. Or two. Just get back to it at the first opportunity.
2. Feel free to abbreviate. The days you get home late, read a Psalm and pray. At least pray.
3. Make Bible time a priority. Ignore the phone. It reminds your children they are important and this time is valuable. This is pleasant, quality time with your children. It is your opportunity to relax together.
4. Have everyone participate. This is just as enriching for the parent as for the children.
5. Add variety to this family time. And don't be concerned if Bible time consistently falls back into a familiar pattern.

   + Play a Bible based game. I invented a *Books of the Bible* game we still play (available on my Web site, http://peggysuewells .com).
   + Have sword drills—race to see who can find Scripture references first.
   + Watch a Bible-based DVD such as Focus on the Family's series titled *That the World May Know*.
   + Read about a missionary or other person of faith.
   + On Palm Sunday, reenact Jesus' triumphal entry. One kid pretends to be the donkey and the others take turns riding on the donkey's back.
   + On Christmas morning, have the children place the figures into the Nativity scene as you read aloud the Christmas story.

6. Allow young children to use this as cuddle time. Sitting on your lap is good practice for sitting in church later. Wiggly children may like to color, sort socks, do hand sewing, brush the dog, or quietly build with Legos while listening.

7. Remember that all questions are good questions. A great many questions naturally get answered during the process of exploring and learning what the Bible says.

8. Once a child is comfortable reading the Bible, encourage them to read a chapter daily for personal devotions. And then encourage journaling. I suggest the children write a sentence summarizing what the chapter was about. If there is a word in the chapter they don't know, they look it up and copy the definition. Then copy a favorite verse or write a prayer. From there, journaling seems to take on a life of its own.

The goal of family devotions is to introduce our children to the Savior, Jesus Christ. Becoming a member of God's eternal family is surprisingly easy. "If you confess with your mouth, 'Jesus is Lord,' and believe in your heart that God raised him from the dead, you will be saved. For it is with your heart that you believe and are justified, and it is with your mouth that you confess and are saved" (Rom. 10:9–10).

My son found comfort in memorizing that Scripture. It's the answer when you question your relationship with the Lord. It's the answer when your child asks how to become a Christian.

The benefits of this time include stability for the children, a forum for questioning, a safe place for expressing hurt and hope, and an easy family tradition.

The church is a support for you and me. It is a supplement. But the real responsibility of helping our children and ourselves have a genuine spiritual walk lies with us. As parents, it is vital to introduce our children to the Lord. I am convinced that if I don't do my part to introduce my children to their Creator today, I have missed my greatest opportunity.

Begin today. Begin by investing just seven minutes.

◁ Look Back

What aspect of parenting do you feel is the most essential? Looking at your daily schedule, are you giving priority to what you believe is most important? What are your feelings about reading the Bible with your children?

▷ Move Ahead

What will you introduce today for family Bible time? "The ordinances of the LORD are sure and altogether righteous. They are more precious than gold, than much pure gold; they are sweeter than honey, than honey from the comb" (Ps. 19:9–10). In honor of this truth, we habitually enjoy Bible time and dessert simultaneously. Scripture and hot fudge sundaes are a fabulous combination.

> Your word is a lamp to my feet
> and a light for my path.
>
> PSALM 119:105

CHAPTER 8

SAFE IN THE BRICK HOUSE

Where do I connect and belong?

Let us hold unswervingly to the hope we profess, for he
who promised is faithful. And let us consider how we
may spur one another on toward love and good deeds.
Let us not give up meeting together, as some are in the
habit of doing, but let us encourage one another—and
all the more as you see the Day approaching.

HEBREWS 10:23–25

It was winter outside and it was winter in my soul when I made the
trip to another town to say good-bye to a special friend.

Cold and wet, I followed the funeral party to a local church. Though
it was not a Sunday, the doors were open, the lights were on, and it
was warm inside. I was welcomed into the fellowship hall and given a
seat, and people I didn't know fed me a hot, home-cooked meal.

That church was not my church. It was not the church my family
attended. Most of the mourners did not attend that church. Many of
those who came to remember my friend don't attend church at all.
We were all welcomed just the same. On a difficult day, that local

congregation of believers nurtured our bodies and nurtured our souls.

Right now, you are emotionally cold and wet. A guest at the funeral of your marriage. What comfort to be gathered in by a community and welcomed to a place where the doors are open, the light is on, it is warm inside, and there is a seat for you.

Inside the church, your body and soul will be nourished.

The sad truth is that many churches are quick to embrace a divorced woman who comes to church and accepts Christ as her Lord but congregations are not always sure what to do with a church member who experiences a divorce. There is an unspoken belief that if we are spiritual enough, our marriages will survive; if we remain in abusive marriages, we will win him with our silent acceptance; that a husband's ill treatment of his wife and family is triggered by her lack of deference and if she is merely more submissive to a bully, he will morph into a gentleman.

When my marriage was crumbling, popular Christian marriage books as well as fellow churchgoers preached that a devout wife should serve an unfaithful husband his favorite dinner and confess her faults and shortcomings that drove him to an affair. Then seduce him with a new nightie. No kidding. It was a great deal for the guy.

As if women who are familiar with relationship challenges haven't already tried that. Multiple times. Rewarding dishonoring behavior only encouraged further abuse and made me feel like a failure.

I confess. Prior to my own experience, I was judgmental of others who found themselves suddenly single. I believed that if someone just followed the biblical formula, their marriage would remain blissfully intact. That was before I understood that no one can control another person. One spouse may be committed to the path of happily-ever-after while the other decides to go a drastically different direction. One spouse may be doing the dos of Scripture while the other may behave completely contrary to the wedding vows. Both spouses may choose to violate and destroy the foundation of the marriage covenant.

While some single women have received support from their church, others have been shunned.

"Why would anyone want to separate or divorce," my friend sagely noted, "unless being married is worse than being alone?"

"My first husband left and my second husband died," an older friend concurred. "Both were terribly hard but I will tell you that of the two, death is easier."

"The church is weak in dealing with women who are divorced," my counselor said.

The church will have to deal with this issue because you and I are part of the congregation and we are far from alone. Studies repeatedly show that for regular churchgoers, the likelihood of a marriage ending in divorce is identical to those who do not attend.[1]

It's a catch-22 for a woman in the church. While my pastor and counselor agreed that I must look after the safety of my children and myself, the church distanced themselves from me when the marriage separated. I was judged a bad mother if my children were in a threatening situation. I was judged a bad wife if I couldn't make my marriage work.

I don't advocate church-hopping—finding a new church each time I am offended or something doesn't go my way. A church is for putting down roots to grow deep in relationship, both with the Lord and with a spiritual family who boasts a bumper crop of foibles and irritable habits. Just like me. But in the case where judgment and legalism are no longer balanced by grace, it may be better to find a new congregation who accepts and supports me and my children in our altered state. We are grown-ups; we are big enough to acknowledge gracelessness exists, and we can ask God to help us to be full of grace in our own attitudes toward others.

When I was in grade school, my parents divorced. The church we attended viewed divorce as the unforgivable sin and corporately stopped speaking to my mother. Each week she left the church more wounded for having come. Though it wasn't long before she stopped attending, I continued to walk to Sunday school each weekend. I clung to this stability in my chaotic environment. But after months of being ignored, one Sunday I walked the mile home in an October rain while—warm, dry, and belonging—the people I attended church with drove past. I didn't go back.

Why should you and I give up a perfectly good Sunday, maybe our only day to sleep in, to attend church? Jesus went to synagogue on the Sabbath, and if ever a person had good reason not to go, he did! When he went he set the example to teach and encourage others.

Being involved in a supportive church is essential. In our situation, we seek rest and connection, security and belonging. Jesus promises rest for our spirit. Refreshing rest is a result of accepting the forgiveness Christ offers, being confident that heaven is my home, and—unlike other faiths—knowing that nothing can separate me from God's love. Whatever happens, my future is secure.

The local church exists as a place to connect and belong. The foundation that brings us together is our relationship in Christ Jesus. I am drawn to him because he embodies and epitomizes love, forgiveness, and grace. Especially grace. All the character traits of the Lord are winsome, but my favorite is grace. The leadership of Jesus Christ is not characterized by rules, rigidity, or senseless demands. His gentle, quiet voice soothes and guides.

Having the same Heavenly Father, we are a family. Like a weekly family reunion, church is a place to come together to be thankful, to pray, and to learn more about God. Gathering as a spiritual family, we care about and support each other. The church is an asset, a tool, a community, a fellowship, and a resource. Together we bring glory to God through worship, fellowship, community, evangelism, prayer, Bible study, Christian education, and outreach to the community and the world.

When I belong to a church, I partner with others, corporately accomplishing more than I can do alone. My monetary contributions are pooled with the donations of others into a greater, more effective amount. In this larger circle, my efforts, ideas, and time are increased when combined with what others bring to the equation. Through this partnership, I can have a multiplied impact on others, greater than I might have on my own.

When seeking a church home, I like to visit three times. A single visit might fall on a high week or a low week, but three visits can provide me with an idea of the personality of the congregation and the church's teaching style. I also ask for the church's statement of faith. I have met the nicest folks and been drawn to their church, only to find through the statement of faith that we are polarized in our beliefs.

The greatest challenge of being part of a church is getting along with others. People in the church are not perfect. "It is not the healthy who need a doctor, but the sick," Jesus said (Matt. 9:12). On first impression, everything usually appears to be running well. After further involvement, we will find that there are issues, just like in any other family. Welcome to reality.

As we experienced firsthand, getting along with people can be challenging. People have opposing opinions, methods, and motivations. And, even when we speak the same language, there can be miscommunication.

A great church studies Scripture and helps people know Jesus Christ. A great church encourages questions and has leaders who are open and accountable. A great church develops leadership skills in individuals in the congregation and does not place a higher value on leaders than on those who are led. A great church prepares "God's people for works of service, so that the body of Christ may be built up" (Eph. 4:12).

At church we celebrate Jesus and his resurrection. We go to help and be helped by those who are on the same spiritual journey, greeting others and making them feel at home. In church, my children and I have a place to put down roots in our community. "Remember the Sabbath day by keeping it holy," says Exodus 20:8. God gave us one day a week to rest, refresh, reflect, relax, read, enjoy music, and converse with God and others. Taking an hour to sit still, to sing, and hear God's Word is a great way to "be still, and know that I am God" (Ps. 46:10). Church is a place to worship the Father, the Son, and the Holy Spirit.

Ultimately church is not about us; it is all about God. As long as I have my eyes on fellow human beings, I will certainly be disappointed. Anyone who leans on me will be disappointed. Eventually I will let them down. Not on purpose, but I am only a woman. The only One worthy of our devotion is our Lord.

"After looking out over the congregation each week and judging the people as they sang," described Tom, the drummer on our church worship team, "God reminded me that he told me not to judge but to love."

Each of us is in process. I make mistakes. So do others in the congregation. Each time, we merely prove that we are human and need a Savior. In the same way that I want people to extend gentleness and grace to me when I am not perfect, I must do the same for them. When we do this well, we are applying "relationship glue" so that even when one of us does something stupid, anyone can make their way back to reconnect.

When you and I belong to Jesus Christ, we belong to his body and to his worldwide church. Every person in church has similar needs to connect and belong. I worship where I worship not because it's perfect but because it's where God wants me as part of a local family. A weekly appointment together with God and his children is therapeutic.

Eating a balanced diet is on our list of healthy things to do. We will drive quite a distance to dine at a favorite restaurant. I propose that it merits the drive to church each Sunday to get spiritually fed. For eight years my family attended a church that was a half hour away. People asked why we drove so far. It was worth every minute to be involved in that congregation that was fired up for the Lord and reaching out into the community.

In John 14:1–2, Jesus said he was going to prepare a place for us. Someday he'll come back and take us to heaven. To our real home. Nothing, including the church we attend, will be perfect in this life. Even so, the local assembly of believers is a preparation for the heaven that will one day be our eternal address.

Once you and I settle our future by accepting Jesus Christ as Lord, we are a Christian, a Christ-follower. The local church is our family, our haven, and our home on earth. The paralytic's friends knew where to find Jesus. They knew what Jesus could do. They had faith for the paralytic. And they were prepared to find a way, even it if meant making a hole in the roof to get their friend to Jesus and his healing. Those friends are a picture of the church.

"You are the light of the world. A city on a hill cannot be hidden. Neither do people light a lamp and put it under a bowl. Instead they put it on its stand, and it gives light to everyone in the house. In the same way, let your light shine before men, that they may see your good deeds and praise your Father in heaven," Jesus said (Matt. 5:14–16).

The church my family attended for nearly a decade before relocating across the country had a figurative welcome mat out for their community. Whenever a group needed a facility for an event or meeting, they could call our church. A request was refused only if the activity was sinful or if the building was already booked for that date. Scout groups, Weight Watchers, exercise clubs, 4-H clubs, and homeschool organizations met at the building. On almost any day you could drive by the church and see the doors open and the lights on.

"One day I'm going to stand before the Lord," the pastor said, "and he'll ask what I did with the church building he put in my stewardship. I want to say that the church, like the woman at the well in John 4:29, invited the community to 'Come, see a man. . . . Could this be the Christ?'"

Life is challenging. Everyone will experience a winter of the soul. Inside the church, the door is open, the light is on, it is warm, and there is a seat for you and me. Inside the church, our bodies and our souls will be nourished. Someone in the church will tell us about salvation and forgiveness. Someone will tell us about grace and mercy. Someone will tell us about Jesus Christ.

> Let the peace of Christ rule in your hearts, since as members of one body you were called to peace. And be thankful. Let the word of Christ dwell in you richly as you teach and admonish one another with all wisdom, and as you sing psalms, hymns and spiritual songs with gratitude in your hearts to God. And whatever you do, whether in word or deed, do it all in the name of the Lord Jesus, giving thanks to God the Father through him.
>
> Colossians 3:15–17

◁ Look Back

Search out and highlight all the "I am's" Jesus said about himself in Scripture.

▷ Move Ahead

Practice gentleness and grace, both in and out of church.

> The Christian life is not just a private affair of your own. If we are born again into God's family, not only has he become our Father but every other believer in the world, whatever his nation or denomination, has become our brother or sister in Christ. . . . But it is no good supposing that membership in the universal church of Christ is enough; we must belong to some local branch of it. . . . Every Christian's place is in a local church, sharing in its worship, fellowship and witness.
>
> JOHN STOTT, *BASIC CHRISTIANITY*

CHAPTER 9

A Pea Under the Mattress

Do I have to forgive?

I lift up my eyes to the hills—
where does my help come from?
My help comes from the LORD,
the Maker of heaven and earth.
He will not let your foot slip—
he who watches over you will not slumber;
indeed, he who watches over Israel
will neither slumber nor sleep.
The LORD watches over you—
the LORD is your shade at your right hand;
the sun will not harm you by day,
nor the moon by night.
The LORD will keep you from all harm—
he will watch over your life;
the LORD will watch over your coming
and going both now and forevermore.

PSALM 121

"Close your eyes and envision Jesus on the cross," the speaker said. "That crown of thorns, those nails in his hands are there because of my sin."

She continued. "Imagine your father or your husband turning his back on you and your child." She paused. "I can't imagine it."

I could. That's my reality.

It is also probably the closest I will come to understanding how Jesus Christ felt when he was betrayed.

There are days when the emotional pain and overwhelming responsibilities are so crushing it feels like I can't breathe. I can take an aspirin for a headache. There is no aspirin for a heartache.

My friend described, "My kids and I are still in the grieving process. Some experts give timetables as to how long each stage of grief should last but those things aren't measured in that manner. Each of us has differences, yet some similarities in the way that we mourn. If we can learn to mourn well, we will live and love well."

This same woman established a support group.

I have been taught that we must grieve all of our losses. Our group exists in part because women have not had a place or taken the time to learn to grieve and to mourn, and there's a difference between the two. I sometimes tell women, "Blessed are those that mourn for they shall be comforted." Jesus has something special for me and for those who will allow themselves to learn to mourn. I cannot receive comfort until I mourn. Personally, I would rather skip that part and be done with it. It's like wearing a sticky, wet piece of clothing that clings to my skin. Panicked, I want to take it off. I struggle to get it off until I tire of the struggle, but I must stop struggling and allow that clothing to dry on me. Before all this happened, I had read Isaiah 61 many times, praying, "Lord, teach me how to comfort all those who mourn." Jesus is answering that prayer. As I comfort others, I must also allow myself to mourn.

I recall days when I circled the bed and laid back down. How could I be so exhausted? A counselor shared that grief work and mourning exact a toll emotionally, physically, spiritually, and financially. It is also a time of growing, resting, learning, and yielding. Like deep muscle exercise, this was all sorts of good, deep stuff.

If we didn't travel through this journey, we wouldn't be real. If we weren't occasionally terrified of what's ahead, then we'd be artificial. There is a treasured richness Jesus can teach us as we journey through depression.

I wish I could offer you a timetable, a calendar with days to cross off. But this time has different lengths for different people. Plod on. You can't get over, under, or around the pain. It's better to walk through the emotional desert to the Promised Land than to set up housekeeping in the airless wasteland.

A pivotal part of the grief process is connected to forgiveness. Surrendering to forgiveness is the fastest way I know out of the life-draining clutches of this emotional vampire known as depression. A resistance to forgive extends our time in the pit.

In the Greek, *forgiveness* means to release or free oneself from something that ensnares. An offense is like the bait stick of a trap. The only way out of the trap is through forgiveness.

 Unforgiveness is the bind that ties—chokes and contorts, poisons and paralyzes. Forgiveness releases, straightens, and energizes. Forgiveness is a willingness to bear the pain. When we choose to forgive, we meet the pain head on.

Jane Rubietta

Whether my past makes me or breaks me depends on how I respond. My past can become the most powerful influence in my life, controlling and programming me for failure. I can keep reaching back into the past and using it as an excuse for present behavior. Or I can use all of those experiences, both good and bad, as a springboard to growth, life, and liberty.

The topic of forgiveness triggers strong emotional responses. People get defensive, aggressive, apologetic, and agitated. As one woman put it, "I put up with his abuse, then I dealt with his cruelty through the divorce. Now I have to forgive the bum too? Why do I have to do it all?"

Getting clarity about what forgiveness is and what it is not eliminates the unnecessary emotion.

 Not to forgive imprisons me in the past and locks out all potential for change. I thus yield control to another, my enemy, and doom myself to suffer the consequences of the wrong. I once heard an immigrant rabbi make an astonishing statement. "Before coming to America, I had to forgive Adolf Hitler," he said. "I did not want to bring Hitler inside me to my new country."

Philip Yancey, *What's So Amazing About Grace?*

Forgiveness is not blind injustice. Never does forgiveness condone the actions of the person who hurt you. It does not stamp what happened as acceptable. Forgiveness never tolerates abuse nor gives the offender permission to continue hurting you or other victims. Forgiveness is not remaining in an abusive marriage or allowing our children to spend unsupervised time with a relative who is a child molester. It is not excusing a husband's affairs, addictions, or abuse. Forgiveness does not allow a serial murderer to go free to kill again and it does not release an offender from the consequences of his or her actions.

Forgiveness is our choice. Not dependent on circumstances or another person, we are powerful when we choose to forgive. "You speak to the Lord every day, saying, 'I choose to forgive, Father.' One day it's gone. That person no longer defines who you are," described

Hee Haw star Lulu Roman. No longer ladies-in-waiting, we need never wait for, "I am sorry. Will you forgive me?" Most people who offend you will never ask for forgiveness. Our offender has no power over our choices. You and I can choose to forgive because we have been forgiven.

Forgiveness is unnatural. Seeking revenge is my natural human response. You and I are Christlike when we forgive. Forgiveness has nothing to do with being logical or fair. Derived from the word *gift*, we give forgiveness with no expectations of the receiver. Forgiveness of grievous life-changing offenses does not make sense to the world.

Forgiveness is a process. Particularly grievous offenses may take more time to heal. The support of family, friends, and often professional counselors help me honestly look at my pain and release it. Though Corrie ten Boom had forgiven the Secret Service officer who assaulted her in the Nazi concentration camp, she continued to be haunted by hideous memories. When Corrie sought the advice of her pastor, he pointed to the church bell. Even after the rope of the bell was no longer pulled, the sound of the bell echoed for some time. The intensity of our painful memories winds down like the church bell.

Forgiveness is not denial. Lasting forgiveness is based on honesty. I must fully acknowledge the pain and betrayal that I have suffered before healing can begin.

Forgiveness is not forgetting. Experiences are chemically burned into our memories, where they remain. As Carolyn Koons stated, "Becoming a Christian did not erase my past. It allowed me to remember my past and deal with it."[1]

Forgiveness is releasing. It is taking the debt the offender owes me and transferring it over to God. Now the offender owes God rather than owing me. I let the two of them deal with it. Forgiveness prevents my abuser from having power over me and frees me from being sabotaged by my past. In this freedom, I am a balanced, cheerful mother and enjoy my own company. "If you keep on biting and devouring each other, watch out or you will be destroyed by each other" (Gal. 5:15).

"News flash," my friend shared. "My ex wrote me a letter of deep apology saying that if he had it to do over, he would certainly do it differently. Asked me to forgive him. And I was able, from my heart, to write back and tell him I forgave him long ago."

Forgiveness heals the forgiver. While I may think forgiveness is a gift I give to the one who hurt me, surprisingly, it is a grand contribution I give to myself and to my children. "He that cannot forgive others breaks the bridge over which he must pass himself," said Thomas Fuller, "for every man has need to be forgiven."

Forgiveness does not guarantee reconciliation. Forgiveness is about me and takes only one person. Reconciliation is about both parties and requires movement from both sides. "Forgiveness depends on *me*; reconciliation depends upon *us*."[2] While many forgivers experience this full circle of restoration, others certainly do not. A wife who fears for her safety and the safety of her children cannot reconcile with an abusive husband. In the case of abandonment and divorce, we can forgive our offender. That part is up to us. That is within our power to do. Reconciliation requires action from the other person. Reconciliation is not always wise, particularly when emotional or physical safety is at risk.

Forgiveness is a lifestyle. It takes time to heal. Often the more grievous the offense, the more time is required to experience forgiveness. "Forgiveness must be taught and practiced, as one would practice any difficult craft."[3] The most content people I know have lives characterized by a continual attitude of forgiveness and being prepared to forgive. Forgiveness spills over into all our relationships. After forgiving abusive husbands, wives often experience forgiveness of their abusive fathers and neglectful mothers.

Forgiveness is not a formula. Ranging from simple to complex, the process of forgiveness is as individual as the people involved. Lewis Smedes put it this way, "We cannot erase the past; we can only heal the pain it has left behind. . . . We are never so free as when we reach back into our past and forgive a person who caused us pain."[4]

Forgiveness is not a feeling. Like love, forgiveness is an action. I can act in a forgiving manner when I do not feel forgiveness. I can stop seeking revenge. Choosing to forgive, putting closure to the event transcends and eventually calms my roller-coaster feelings. Forgiveness is not dependent on my emotions. Rather than a sign of weakness, forgiveness is a courageous act of strength.

Forgiveness is not a magic wand. Those who forgive difficult spouses, parents, or children are not promised ideal relationships in the future. A challenging person frequently continues to stir friction.

Forgiveness is something everyone will have opportunity to experience. As long as we are breathing we will be offended and we will offend.[5] Unintentional offenses happen merely because we are human. Other offenses victimize another; they are premeditated, deliberate, and stem from evil intent. Some offenses are easier to forgive than others. Everyone will encounter situations that can only be resolved through forgiveness.

 When we genuinely forgive, we set a prisoner free and then discover that the prisoner we set free is us.

Lewis Smedes, *The Art of Forgiving*

In *Free Yourself to Love*, Jackie Kendall identifies six reasons why we don't forgive:
1. We feel the offense was too great to be forgiven.
2. The offense is a repeated offense.
3. We struggle with the memories of the offense.
4. We want the offender to be sorry, to pay for what was done.
5. The offender never apologized.
6. We are too angry to consider forgiving.[6]

"They are the three A's, the three unforgivable acts of marriage—adultery, addiction, and abandonment," said Mary Ann Froehlich.

"The ones which prompt well-meaning friends to say, 'I would never put up with that. I could never forgive him. Your husband will never change.' What if God had said that about me and walked away from the cross?"[7] Forgiveness is usually the key that turns the lock to personal change granting the freedom to again dream, love, and live passionately. The truth I resist is that I am powerless to change another person. I cannot cause another to feel remorse. I cannot manipulate that person to feel or behave differently. Trust me, I tried.

The only person I can truly affect for change is myself. Changing my patterns, my attitude, and my behavior can be a herculean effort. Or it can occur in a heartbeat. It is a heart shift. How quickly it occurs, and how easily, completely depends on my willingness to surrender to and to embrace the action that grants me peace.

 Get rid of all bitterness, rage and anger, brawling and slander, along with every form of malice. Be kind and compassionate to one another, forgiving each other, just as in Christ God forgave you.
Ephesians 4:31–32

My friend confided, "I tremble a little when one of my children wants to make me the hero of the divorce because I know their dad has a side, too, and that there were areas of my behavior that I am vastly not proud of. If I forgive him, I find I can also forgive me. And then I can move on."

She added, "For myself, I sometimes find that though I thought I was past it, I am still on the forgiveness journey. It won't be fair. It often hurts and it's not always my fault. But I believe the timing will end up being perfect. I will be so much better and the divorce will be part of my legacy, not the tragedy that defines my life. In the grand scheme, this is all part of the process. It is easier when I surrender. Go with it."

Daniel and Joseph of the Old Testament are my favorite forgiveness examples. Joseph was so hated by his older siblings that they wanted to kill him. They settled for selling him into slavery.

Daniel probably watched his parents be killed by a brutal invading army. He was carried off to a foreign land and forced to serve the very man who had decimated his homeland and his family.

Both men thrived.

 Failure to forgive plunges me into darkness, which keeps me from walking with God in His light, (1 John 1:5–7). But something else happens as well; barriers start to be erected between others and myself. I have personally observed in thousands of lives around the world that the wall is usually the size of the anger in their heart.

Gary Smalley

In both instances, these two men pressed into the Lord. They refused to be victims. Refusing to hold grudges or focus on unforgiveness, they acknowledged that God was Lord of their lives and they trusted him to guide, provide, protect, and give a future and a hope. In their places of confinement, including ten years in prison for Joseph and an overnight stay in the lions' den for Daniel, each surrendered his heart to God. These two adhered to godly principles and maintained a positive, hopeful attitude.

 I will repay you for the years the locusts have eaten.

Joel 2:25

Joseph's journey of forgiveness is reflected in the names of his children. "Joseph named his firstborn Manasseh and said, 'It is because God has made me forget all my trouble and all my father's household.'

The second son he named Ephraim and said, 'It is because God has made me fruitful in the land of my suffering'" (Gen. 41:51–52).

In the face of desperate circumstances, Joseph and Daniel dared to trust God. They dared to believe that he loved them whether they felt it or not. Whether their circumstances appeared to reflect that fact or not. This courageous act of the will was a vital component of their winsome outlook that made them appealing to people, and, I suggest, easy material for God to work with.

Doubtless there are occasions when you can relate to the despairing emotions Joseph and Daniel probably experienced. When it feels like we are drowning, whatever is over our heads is under his feet. Whatever we feel is impossible is actually *Him*possible. Especially forgiveness. It is the key to releasing yourself from your own prison, your own lions' den.

 Forgiveness opens the door and compassion walks through it.

Chuck Lynch

◁ Look Back

When did you last laugh? I mean belly laugh, milk coming out your nose kind of laugh? What makes you smile? Our inability to smile and laugh is often symptomatic of a resistance to forgive.

▷ Move Ahead

Plan a mini getaway. Spend a few hours or a day alone with the Lord. Build in time for Scripture reading, quiet listening to the lover of your soul, and an opportunity to laugh.

The longer I live the more convinced I become that life is 10 percent what happens to us and 90 percent how we respond to it. I believe the single most significant decision I can make on a day-to-day basis is my choice of attitude. It is more important than my past, my education, my bankroll, my successes or failures, fame or pain, what other people think of me or say about me, my circumstances, or my position. Attitude keeps me going or cripples my progress. It alone fuels my fire or assaults my hope. When my attitudes are right, there's no barrier too high, no valley too deep, no dream too extreme, no challenge too great for me.

CHARLES R. SWINDOLL, *STRENGTHENING YOUR GRIP*

CHAPTER 10

GUARD AT THE CASTLE GATE

Can I ensure my children's physical safety?

We must be the change we wish to see in the world.

MAHATMA GANDHI

Why is it that we prepare and serve family dinners until the evening when the man of the house is away on business? Then it's leftovers, cereal, or mac and cheese from a box. Now he's on permanent leave but we are still a family.

Can we have healthy, single-parent families? The answer is a resounding *yes!* But it requires consistent effort. Not the news you wanted to hear when you are already running on empty emotionally, physically, spiritually, and often financially. Yet, if you put your effort into anything in your life, investing in your family is the one arena that is hands down more worth it than any other. In this key area you are the only one who can fill the vacuum. No one else can parent your children. Your family is first priority and you are the critical person that makes all the difference in the world.

To the world you are one person. To your children, you are the world.

After all the craziness we wonder, what does a healthy family look like? According to research, healthy families are characterized by:

+ Open communication. There are no family secrets.
+ Good listening skills. Family members are valued and listened to without interruption.
+ Unconditional love and commitment. They trust each other.
+ Appreciation and affection for one another.
+ Respect for one another and the passing on of solid values. They share responsibility for the family and are supportive of each other.
+ A spiritual focus.
+ Special family times and traditions.
+ Skills for dealing effectively with stress and crisis.

Healthy families do not boast an ideal, problem-free lifestyle. Being a single parent is certainly challenging but having a single-parent household is not the deciding factor of family health. How we face that challenge is what makes the difference. Often how we handle the situation depends on the type of support we receive or ask for. Some of us receive positive support. Others don't.

Many grieve the loss of extended family when the dynamic of our nuclear family changes. Several friends have described how much they missed the dear relationships they experienced with those who used to be in-laws. For some, our natural family members reacted by distancing themselves.

Jesus experienced torn relationships too. When he hung dying on the cross he spoke to his close friend, John. "Here is your mother," he said. And to Mary his mother, he said, "Here is your son" (John 19:26).

In the midst of intense physical agony that I can't begin to imagine, one of Jesus' final and completely human acts was to arrange for the care and provision of his mother. His younger half brothers were not in fellowship with Jesus. Just prior to his fateful arrival in Jerusalem on Palm Sunday, his brothers had mocked him.

Jesus put the care of Mary into the gentle and capable hands of his beloved friend John. He places us in a spiritual family with a rich heritage. As Christ followers, you and I are related to such Hall of Faith nobles as Boaz, Queen Esther, Daniel, Deborah, and the two Josephs—Joseph of the Old Testament and Joseph of the New Testament.

In my home is a plaque that reads, "Friends are the relatives we choose for ourselves." Jesus chose his inner circle and populated it with men such as John, a friend closer than his brothers who he knew would tenderly care for his mother's physical, emotional, and spiritual needs. I believe that at that point in Jesus' earthly life, Mary was his closest family relationship and Jesus was diligent to see to her well-being.

We, too, need to diligently see to the well-being of those in closest family relationship to us. As guardians for our children it is vital we secure a living trust that assures our children will be raised in a place where they will be safe and nurtured—physically, emotionally, and spiritually—should something happen to us. Prayerfully make this decision.

In the case of our untimely death, it may be that the children will be safe going to their father. For some, there are beloved relatives who will easily fill that role. Relatives would be the first option as they provide our children with a sense of family and connection to their heritage.

For others, like Jesus, we have to look outside our extended family to those friends who are closer than family.

One day I will stand alone before the Lord and he will ask what I did with the precious children he placed in my care. My goal is to answer that I did my best to see to their safety and to protect them from any dangers the Lord made known to me. We are only responsible for the information we know. If I know that an individual struggles with an addiction to drugs, alcohol, pornography, or anger; that would not be a safe person to entrust with the care of my children. Not on a temporary basis in terms of babysitting or child care, or for long-term guardianship. Even if that particular person is the next closest relative. Even if not choosing that person makes family members angry. My first responsibility is to my God and my children, not to please men or demanding relatives.

 He tends his flock like a shepherd: He gathers the lambs in his arms and carries them close to his heart; he gently leads those that have young.

Isaiah 40:11

◁ Look Back

Who in your circle of extended family and friends can best serve as loving guardians for your children?

▷ Move Ahead

Finalize a living trust for your children that provides a healthy, competent, nurturing, and godly caretaker for your children in case you are not available to do the job.

Be strong and courageous. Do not be terrified;
do not be discouraged, for the LORD your God
will be with you wherever you go.

JOSHUA 1:9

CHAPTER 11

Equip Your Fairy Godmother

Can I nurture my children's emotional health?

If you bungle raising your children, I don't think
whatever else you do well matters very much.

For the children and you, life can feel like your home has been picked up by the unjolly green giant and shaken until everything is as completely topsy-turvy as Sunday's scrambled eggs. Things that parents promised they would never do, they did. Things children were certain would never be said were probably yelled. When the family foundation is eroded, mothers can feel our relationships with our children are based on our performance.

After making fools of themselves, I've seen too many parents engage in a perpetual competition for "parent who gives the most expensive toys," or "parent who demands the least amount of chores or responsibility from the children," or "parent who rescues the child most often," or "parent who provides the most junk food," or "parent who will always disagree with the other parent's household rules." These situations have nothing to do with what is best for the children and everything to do with being vengeful to an ex-spouse. Sadly, no amount of talking or pleading will convince an unreasonable person to suddenly become reasonable.

It is in this unsettled climate that mothers feel inadequate and lack confidence in their parenting. Complicating the situation may be an unsupportive ex-spouse who tells your child that if he or she is not happy at Mom's, well, there is always the opportunity to threaten to move to Dad's.

Though we feel insecure, this is the exact time when children benefit from a mom who is confident, nurturing, loving, strong, and consistent in her parenting. An environment of healthy structure and affectionate security is a healing balm for regrouping, moving forward, and thriving. For the children. And for us moms. The only way out of the ridiculous games is not to play.

One of my sage counselors said:

> You may see repeated times of intense emotion. It may be all over the page as the kids may have major unresolved issues with their father. Feelings of misplaced guilt, abandonment, abuse, anger, depression, jealousy with one another, frustration, grief, mourning of what was and what was not, desire to control others in order to reduce their own misplaced guilt, and on and on. We can't control those events and it is easy to try and blame someone or something in order to try and make sense out of the senseless.
>
> With each of us it is a different story, yet there are common themes. Sharing together, praying with and for each other, guiding kids who want their dads. We can develop a stronger relationship with Jesus our source of strength, our comfort, and model that to our kids. We can teach our kids how to love and to set boundaries, how to develop strong, safe relationships outside of the family, as the family members become so very stressed and stretched.

I certainly don't have all of the answers to life yet I do know relationships are everything. A strong relationship with Jesus, and a strong relationship with safe people, and strong relationships within the family, if they will let you, are the only things that matter.

When you find yourself struggling to connect with a child or going nose-to-nose with a challenge that is over your head, utilize a competent counselor for yourself and your children. Ask around to find a counselor who has been beneficial to others. Your church may be able to recommend someone.

I had several years of experience working with counselors. After kissing too many frogs—the list was long and distinguished—I met a prince of a counselor. With no less than six degrees, Joe was on staff with a large church. The beauty of this system was that he held a salaried position. His income was not dependent on returning clients. The professionals in this office were motivated to purely minister. I wish every counselor could focus on ministry as he did and that every client could find such a professional.

Establishing comfortable visitation routines with choices for the children is challenging but vital. Most visitation laws do not give children any voice, and that sets up our children to be victims. It teaches them that they have no choice when someone tells them what they must do whether they want to or not. Whether being with someone is beneficial or harmful. Studies show that girls grow up to marry bullies because they are used to being told what to do without regard for their preferences. Boys often grow up and bully like they have seen modeled. The cycle perpetuates.

One friend's ex-husband sexually abused her daughters. Charges were filed with the police. The divorce judge gave the father supervised visits and a six-week anger management course prior to instating normal visitation standards. The court ordered the mother to release the children to him for his state-mandated visits. She was told that if she did not send the children, she would be held in contempt of court and would go to jail. It was his right to see the children. Each weekend that the girls spent the night with their dad, they tied a string that linked their wrists together so that if one was woken in the night, it would wake the other. That was how they protected each other from further abuse.

Current situations like these keep women and children bound in toxic relationships. Laws that protect the rights of violent and abusive men are not protecting innocent children. Women have a difficult, if not impossible time protecting their children in the face of such legislation.

The balance comes in providing opportunities for children to have a healthy relationship with their father in an environment where they are respected and permitted to respectfully voice their feelings and opinions.

In high school, my best friend was Marti. Her parents, like mine, had divorced when it wasn't particularly fashionable. Her father, Will, remains the best example of fathering while not in the home that I've ever seen. Though Will lived an hour away, he treated Marti's mother with kindness and respect. He offered to help and fill in with the children wherever she needed support. He didn't push, demand, or bully. It was never about his rights and was always about nurturing, providing for, and loving his children.

Marti's mom moved to an apartment near our school and she returned to work. After school each day, Marti's dad called, asked about school, and coached Marti on her homework. When she wanted to buy a car, Will arranged and paid for a safety inspection, new tires, and regular maintenance. Every other weekend he invited Marti and her boyfriend, now husband, to his home where they enjoyed time together. When Marti married, her dad was a second pair of experienced eyes as they considered which home to purchase. Looking to their future, he began and oversaw their investment portfolio and paid for the couple and their children to come on yearly vacations.

He gently parented Marti without being spiteful to her mother. Never demanding, he proved himself trustworthy as a father and created a lifelong relationship with his daughter, her husband, and his grandchildren. Will behaved like a mature, caring adult. He took responsibility to develop and maintain a benevolent parent relationship with his daughter. He gave love, guidance, finances, and time without attaching strings of obligation. Marti knew she could count on him.

Sadly, Marti's story is all too rare. More often, divorced parents continue to hate each other more deeply than they ever loved each other. Resentment, resistance, revenge, bitterness, manipulation, and harrying are more common than not. The stress level is constantly at a fevered pitch and the children keep adding lousy memories to their childhood.

Christians sometimes exhibit the ugliest breakups. After turning the other cheek again and again as bad behavior escalates, by the time a spouse declares that enough is enough, the situation is exceedingly venomous.

There are plenty of arguments debating whether a bad dad is better than no dad. Is it better for a child to have communication with an abusive or addictive father? If a father abandons his child, should the mother track him down and force him to have visits with his child? Should a mother pursue a father who abandons his family and pressure him to financially support his children? What about the father who demands visitation but doesn't provide financial support?

One of the greatest gifts we give our young ones is their own voice. Equipping youth with a balance of respect for others, a deep sense of personal responsibility, and the strength to be true to themselves is no small task. This is easier to accomplish when divorced parents are mindful of maintaining a nurturing environment for the children. It is, at best, challenging when one or both parents are angry, bitter, vengeful, and selfish. In that scenario, the children's needs are ignored and the children are too often used as pawns in spiteful conquests.

When it comes to call nights and visitations, the physical and sexual safety of the children is the first consideration. Their emotional safety is every bit as important but not something the courts are adept at considering. Often the spouse who has left is inconsistent with parenting skills, keeping their word, maintaining their finances, and following through with family responsibilities, which is why families are separated in the first place. That inconsistency continues, causing further instability. Attorneys and family agencies observe that many inconsistent fathers eventually drift off to pursue a new life. In any event, we want to avoid an emotional tug-of-war between warring parents over the affection or control of the children. We don't want to leverage the children in an attempt to control an ex-spouse.

Circumstances get complicated quickly and I won't begin to offer pat answers. I wish there were some. I could have used a few. The best solution is to stay calm and keep out of the emotional drama that accomplishes nothing more than making adults look dreadfully immature.

A gentle answer turns away wrath, but a harsh word stirs up anger.

Proverbs 15:1

I'm not advocating allowing children to be rude and dictate policy for adults. I am saying they should be heard. When a child feels uncomfortable with arrangements, listen without interruption and see if something can be adjusted so the child feels safe and secure.

You are the mom. Take confidence in the fact that God gave these children to you because he knows you are the best one to mother them. Listen to your children and allow them to make choices when you can. When you are conflicted, seek counsel from a qualified counselor and a good support team made up of people who care deeply about you and your children. Get feedback from them. But in the end you are still the mom, and the final decision is yours. Trust yourself to make good decisions for you and your children.

 Our tendency is to be interested in something that is growing in the garden, not in the bare soil itself. But if you want to have a good harvest, the most important thing is to make the soil rich and cultivate it well.

Shunryu Suzuki

◁ Look Back

What are your send-off traditions when your children visit their father and his side of the family?

▷ Move Ahead

Like a supple tree bends in a strong wind, make the simple (not easy) effort to be flexible, allowing the strong emotions of the situation to blow past.

The future is not some place we are going to, but one we are creating. The paths to it are not found but made, and the activity of making them changes both the maker and the destination.

JOHN SCHAAR

CHAPTER 12

THERE'S NO PLACE LIKE HOME

How do I make home sweet?

In quietness and confidence shall be your strength.

ISAIAH 30:15 NKJV

D id you have fun?"

"Hummm hum," is the usual mumbled reply.

They want me to ask, to be interested. When the children return home after visiting with their dad, they often feel awkward about the situation. And rightly so. This is not how family life is supposed to go, how it is supposed to look. They are pleased about the question and are sometimes unsure how to answer.

If they did have a good time, will that news be painful to Mom? If it was unpleasant, will that be hurtful because I was not able to protect them from another negative experience? Suddenly the children recognize that their parents strongly react to what they share. It can mean the difference between a relaxed day and a tense one. It is a huge load for a child to carry.

Can the children trust the questions of their parents? Is the question because the parent is interested in the child? Or is the parent digging for information to wield against the ex-spouse? Should they invite a friend to come along and have fun? Or will that friend be subjected to drama and interrogating questions?

A child's social life should not be completely altered because of visitations. If the parents were together, the child would continue lessons, sports, summer camp, and friends. Visits can be made around these events or the weekend parent can keep the child's scheduled commitments.

Send children for their visitation with a smile and wishes for a great time. Set them up for success and eliminate the guilt they naturally feel for leaving you behind. Welcome them home with a warm embrace and the gift of decompression time.

I fight my own anger and bitterness when they are away visiting their dad. What a strange state of affairs when the only one not invited, not included, is the mother. What happened to that promise to love, honor, and cherish? That vow made before God, family, and friends degenerated into expensive attorneys and court orders that take my babies from their mother for periods of time.

It left me contemplating. *What am I called to do?* I watch a young mother care for her toddler and my eyes fill with tears as I yearn to be with my own babies. When they are pulled away for these times, life races past like a train and I stand still watching the blurred figures of people with purpose on their way to their destiny.

Sidelined like the traveler without a ticket who twitches with desire to engage, I show up to eagerly catch a glimpse through the windows. And life speeds by, populated with those who knew how to get on the train and those who at least made friends and lasting marriages with travelers who reached out and pulled them aboard. Bursting with ambition and longing, I view the speeding train, having no idea where to find the station to get on. I sit on the bench, unnoticed, watching real players in the game of life.

Then the children come home and it feels like family again. Rich and full. Connected. Belonging. Rooted. Creative and messy. Serious and hilariously funny. Deep and witty. Fruits and vegetables and our famous homemade brownies and floss your teeth and yes you can stay up fifteen more minutes. It's "Für Elise" perpetually played on the piano; hot chocolate made with cocoa, honey, cinnamon, and ginger every morning; dishes piled in the sink because no one puts them in the dishwasher; mounds of laundry we affectionately refer to as Mt. Never-rest; chalk on the driveway, playing dollhouse, Dutch Blitz marathons, occasional burp-offs, reading stories aloud, and speaking in movie quotes.

 Happiness will be a crown they will always wear. They will celebrate and shout because all sorrows and worries will be gone far away.
Isaiah 35:10 CEV

"I feel at ease," described my daughter.

"We are a mix of *Little Women* and *The Odd Couple*," my teenager observed.

The best activity for the transition time right after my children returned home from being with their dad was for all of us to relax with a light-hearted comedy video. Careful not to press them with questions, I remain open in case they want to talk. That may be later or even the next day. Sometimes it is days later. Sometimes not at all. It is unnatural and sad when children have deep areas of their lives they don't feel comfortable sharing with parents. Conversely, it is tricky for a mother to nurture a child when there are veiled places the child keeps from us.

The challenging aspect for me is to constantly put on my big girl panties and act like an adult. Several times my older children have pointed out that it was time I did exactly that. That means I must suck it up and take the high road whether I feel like it or not. No, it's not fair. And it's not easy. But it is what is right. For me. And for my children.

"What will you do while we are gone?" This was from the younger children.

"Let me know what you will be doing so I won't worry about you," I heard from my older children. It was the same question, just phrased differently due to their age. They were telling me that they loved me and wanted to know I would be all right when they were away. When we were apart in this unnatural state of family.

Drinking, eating myself stupid, sinking into depression, being foolish with men or other destructive actions was not an option. Tempting, but not an option. Neither productive nor in line with our family standards. I've seen far too many women make those choices. I couldn't do that to my children. I wouldn't do that to myself.

"Submit to one another out of reverence to Christ," instructs Ephesians 5:21. Relationship is rooted in communication, companionship, and mutual submission. It is putting the needs of another before my own. That is precisely what Christ did. He put my needs before his own and met them. For me he humbled himself to the point of death on a cross. His is the love story of a husband, a heavenly bridegroom, who—no matter how often I betray him and cheat on him by preferring recognition or possessions or other relationships—loves me so much that he faithfully pursues me and gave his very life for me. We will celebrate this great love story in the marriage ceremony described in the final chapter of Revelation.

With Christ's example of what to do before me, I discovered that those difficult days were opportune to schedule a hair appointment, enjoy time with a friend, do holiday shopping, or meet with the tax accountant. I used those days to write, attend a conference, visit people and places, teach, and go on retreats. Because we were all uncomfortable in the situation, the children felt better when they knew I was pleasantly occupied. And I was more delightful to come home to when I maintained a positive perspective.

My children fared well when I remained consistent with family standards and confident in my role as their mother. We both needed to trust that I would choose wisely. They needed a mom who was calm and who leaned on the Lord as her Source.

 People are like tea bags—you have to put them in hot water before you know how strong they are.

Anonymous

◁ Look Back

What are your reentry traditions when your children return home after a visit with their father and his side of the family?

▷ Move Ahead

Wisely invest the time the children are away to catch up on rest, refreshment, and interests that make your eyes light up.

The Spirit of the Sovereign LORD is on me,
because the LORD has anointed me
to preach good news to the poor.
He has sent me to bind up the brokenhearted,
to proclaim freedom for the captives
and release from darkness for the prisoners,
to proclaim the year of the LORD's favor
and the day of vengeance of our God,
to comfort all who mourn,
and provide for those who grieve in Zion—
to bestow on them a crown of beauty instead of ashes,
the oil of gladness instead of mourning,
and a garment of praise instead of a spirit of despair.

ISAIAH 61:1–3

CHAPTER 13

THE GHOST OF CHRISTMAS PAST

How do I help my family survive and thrive?

Do not let any unwholesome talk come
out of your mouths, but only what is helpful for building
others up according to their needs, that it may
benefit those who listen.

EPHESIANS 4:29

I've gained and lost 350 pounds. That's 50 pounds with each pregnancy; yes, more than the recommended amount but I'm an over-
achiever. This is substantial material for an eager tabloid reporter
seeking a weighty story and ample weight-loss tips.

When my son's battle buddy began hanging out at our home, he
asked, "Do you have chocolate every day?"

"Don't you?" I handed him a warm brownie fresh from the oven.
"Chocolate is not just for breakfast."

Health experts recommend we eat several servings of fruit daily.
Cocoa beans and coffee beans grow on trees. That makes them a fruit.

Fitness books can be summed up in one principle; move more and eat less. It's good for our health. Regular exercise combined with a healthy diet may be inconvenient when I crave a large bag of vitamin M's (M&Ms) and a parking place on the couch for a movie marathon today, but getting up for aerobics now and fitting into my jeans in the morning is certainly preferable—physically and financially—to chronic disease or bypass surgery in the future.

The same is true in family life. With a little daily effort spiced with generous portions of fun, we can encourage thriving families in a pleasant and nurturing environment.

Within the home, each family develops traditions and rituals. Keep those that are uplifting. Now is a splendid time to drop any with negative memories associated. Introduce new traditions that bring joy and a sense of connectedness for you and your children. At bedtime, read aloud. No matter how old children are, they enjoy a good story and like to be read to. Celebrate large and small victories and holidays.

Resiliency experts have identified positive traits of children and adults who successfully survive crises and challenging life circumstances. The glue that cements strong family bonds is a consistent level of respect, connection, and fun invested daily into relationships. A steady, loving, joyful relationship becomes a constant pattern to be relished during the best of times and counted on during the worst of times.

Occasional thoughtful acts sprinkled throughout the year won't yield positive results. Neither my emotional fuel tank nor my children's can be filled with a stingy eyedropper.

Consistent thoughtfulness wrapped up in longstanding traditions frequently prevents a crisis entirely. Other times these gracious habits help a family survive a catastrophe. In the case of a wrenching upheaval, these familiar and informal rituals anchor relationships with feelings of connecting and belonging through established venues for communicating and working through problems.

Our family Bible time has proved to be a practiced point of connection. On days when a daughter is grumbly, troubled, and distant, I see that child drift into the room as we begin our customary Bible reading. Soon, her body relaxes and she joins with family members in this common space of being together.

On a grander scale, family traditions provide a bridge for estranged family members to cross. Yearly holiday celebrations and family reunions provide a safe opening for that family member who has drifted away, or become offended, to reconnect. It is a natural occasion for family to reach out to a distant relationship. The time to brainstorm about rituals or thoughtful deeds is not *during* a crisis. That's too late. Good habits must already be in place.

 You can spell "love" a thousand different ways.
Virginia Reynolds

Good habits that have served others include:
+ Pray together frequently.
+ Enjoy regular devotions as a family.
+ Encourage and model a personal relationship with the Lord for each family member.
+ Use a respectful tone of voice. Children should be accustomed to being spoken to with respect by their parents. We set the standard and model for our children for how others should respect them and for how our children should show respect.
+ Say yes as often as possible. Be positive and reflect a world of possibility for our children. For those challenging requests, rather than an instantaneous "no," say, "Let's see how we can make this happen."
+ Find opportunities to laugh together.
+ Keep in touch. Communicate. Give your children the security of knowing the schedule, what to expect in the day, where you are, and how to reach you.

+ "Come apart" or you will come apart. Take regular rest and refresh days. Vacations come in all shapes and sizes—from a week away to hot fudge sundaes, a walk, or a jaunt to the park.

Conversely, barriers to a thriving environment are the "unwritten rules" that weasel into our family dynamic. These may have taken root during the turbulent years leading up to divorce or crept in since the breakup. Intentionally root them out as these unofficial rules can scream louder than the verbalized ones and sabotage the nurturing environment we're trying to establish.

1. Communication

"The trash needs to go out," I'd say.

Some time later I would repeat the observation.

By the third time, I was not a happy camper and someone would drag out the trash. "No one ever does anything I want done unless I get angry," I complained.

"If you want one of us to do something," my son suggested, "just say so."

"I said it three times."

"You said the trash needed to go out," he reminded. "That was not a request for someone to take care of it."

Later he told me that the children were well aware of what I wanted and had no intention of doing anything unless asked. "We don't do hints."

The notice for me was that I hinted when I wanted something done. Sure, I had reasons for this—conditioned by years of being told no by my spouse, I harbored beliefs that I was imposing, annoying others with my requests, not worthy of having my needs met, that I might get what I wanted if I hinted or manipulated rather than communicated openly and honestly.

No one should be expected to act on hints. It was healthier for all of us when I communicated clearly as a parent. "Josiah, please take out the trash." Plain, to the point, responsible.

2. Money

Many families have unspoken rules around money. "We can't afford it" and "Money doesn't grow on trees" and "That's too expensive" are clichés that speak volumes when they are the deciding factor for what the children are allowed to do. We quickly teach our children lifelong lessons by how we talk about, handle, and manage money.

Are finances a tool toward creating our lifestyle or is money a strict dictator? Do we live in a spirit of poverty and scarcity? Or do we believe that God owns the cattle on a thousand hills and gives good gifts, increase, and abundance? Am I teaching my children about possibility or limiting all of us to probability?

Positive responses include, "Wow, that's a great goal. How can we make that happen?"

"What ideas do you have to help fund this?"

"Let me think about this."

"No, not now, and thanks for asking."

Abraham, Job, David, and Solomon were abundantly wealthy because God gave them abundance and increase. Lydia and the Proverbs 31 woman were both lucrative businesswomen. Money itself is not evil. It is the love of money—greed—that is evil. Anything we value as more important than God is idolatry.

3. Interaction

Take a close look at how family members interact with each other. Does someone pout to get his or her way? When one family member is angry, do others break a sweat to diffuse the tension? Is the silent treatment a regular practice at your house? Are gifts distributed based on how someone performs? Is one child a favorite, another the scapegoat? Is money used to control? Does a parent buy one child and form an alliance with another?

In addition to noticing the unwritten rules, see what roles family members play. Is there one who is responsible? One who provides comic relief? The dramatic one? The rebellious person? The caretaker?

Most families automatically fall into similar roles. When a cast member decides they no longer want to play that part, the dynamics are upset, drama unfolds, and the others scramble to manipulate the family member back into the familiar pattern so the status quo remains.

The antidote for this circus is to release each other from expectations. Controlling another person is never healthy. Love and support each member of the family to be all they can be in Christ. Relax, extend freedom and grace, and enjoy the development process. The healthiest families I know are ones that do not make demands on each other. Without demands, there are no judgments and no offenses. Within your home, create an environment that is role-free. This begins when the head of the household—me and you—behave like mature adults.

Single parent households are still a family. Most of us are healthy families who share balanced meals in a tidy and cozy setting. We value family time, family members, and enjoy meaningful traditions. Healthy families give each other the security of a safe place to connect and belong.

 Children need more than food, shelter, and clothing. They need at least one person who is crazy about them.

Fran Stott

◁ Look Back

What family traditions are good for your family? What family traditions or unwritten rules are not beneficial for your family?

▷ Move Ahead

Ask each family member what one activity they most like to do on holidays. Ask what activity they most like to do as a family. Adopt a new, fun family tradition.

> There are only two ways to live your life.
> One is as though nothing is a miracle.
> The other is as though everything is a miracle.
>
> ALBERT EINSTEIN

CHAPTER 14

FROM DUCKLINGS TO SWANS

How can I encourage my children?

If you look for the bad in people
expecting to find it, you surely will.

ABRAHAM LINCOLN

In the kitchen, I prepared dinner while I listened to my second-born practice the piano.

"Mama," she called from the living room. "Was Bach a nice man?"

"From what I've read about him," I considered, "I believe he was."

"Good," she said. "Then he won't mind that I'm fixing his music."

Dare to be the parent you dreamed you could be. In the chaos, so much attention goes to what is wrong with the situation that negativity can become a whirling vortex pulling family members deeper into its dark hole. The solution is to focus on the positives. To put our energy into what is right and beautiful in our lives and in each other.

Each of my seven children learns differently. Each has unique interests and passions. Four so far have graduated from high school and college, and gone on to careers. Focusing on their strengths is the most important lesson I learned from our years together. As their strengths became stronger, their weaker skills also improved.

Concentrating on improving weak areas was frustrating for me, and a negative environment for my children. In the middle of the three older girls, Leilani was sandwiched between two outspoken siblings. A verbal processor myself, I realized this quietly artistic child needed another way to communicate. I asked the Lord for guidance and he directed me to music. I phoned the only person I knew in our little town that played piano.

Mary Ann graciously explained she had a waiting list for lessons. "That's fine," I said, naively. "Please add my name to your list."

"It's a two-year list," she cautioned.

"No problem." I was confident that God would take care of the details.

A few days later, Mary Ann telephoned. "I've been praying about this and I can carve out a morning slot on Thursday."

I was ecstatic.

"But," she went on, "it's not for your oldest. It's for your second daughter." In our circle, the oldest child typically began music lessons first, followed by the siblings as they became old enough. When I inquired about lessons, I hadn't specified which daughter I was calling about. In her prayer time, God had given Mary Ann the same message he had given me.

Sitting side by side on the piano bench, teacher and student played music theory games. Mary Ann's practiced fingers and kindred spirit guided Leilani to make beautiful music. I watched and took notes so I could coach Leilani during her daily practice times.

After each lesson, Mary Ann celebrated the wonderful traits she saw in my daughter. She showed me Leilani through fresh, adoring eyes. An accomplished composer and writer, Mary Ann was a specialist in music therapy and children. We became best friends and co-authors because she saw the best in my child.

Throughout their childhood, I introduced the children to a vast menu of experiences and topics, much like throwing cooked spaghetti at a wall and seeing what sticks. As you consider your own children's gifts and abilities, take a look at some of the things that benefited us:

+ We focused on music as an interest the children could pursue together. Over the years, the children added instruments and changed music genres but music remained the common denominator. Other choices might be sports, literature, or raising animals. Two families I know build and race cars while another household is bonkers over table games.

+ Volunteering was part of life from age fourteen until the child got a job or graduated. The children volunteered at the hospital, our large church, 4-H, schools, radio stations, and the Civil Air Patrol. Young people have the ability to impact the world and act as valuable contributors to the community. Serving on advisory boards for groups like Remedy.fm benefited both my teens and these organizations.

+ If we could see and touch something rather than read about it, we did. We went on field trips ranging from local spots to Israel, England, St. Croix, Canada, Nicaragua, and Hawaii.

+ My children accompanied me everywhere from court appearances, to flights, to speaking engagements, to dentist appointments. They learned how to behave in any situation and how to talk to anyone.

Every child quickly outperformed me in some area. The Lord graciously provided mentors or instructors in every field from music to chemistry, from art to sports, from scriptwriting to aeronautics to medicine.

Some children will be prodigies. Others will be generalists—good at multiple skills. But everyone can learn something about any topic or skill.

Loving my children meant being interested in what interested them. It meant loving what they loved. As they explored a myriad of interests and developed their talents, I found myself involved in adventures I might not have otherwise enjoyed.

While our home became an art studio and a dozen other things, it still housed our daily lives. To help my children be responsible in the world, I encouraged them to begin at home:

+ Each child had a daily job to do for the family. Some call it chores. We called it the service we did for each other to keep our family and home functioning. We rotated kitchen clean-up, laundry, vacuuming, breakfast preparation, and caring for pets. If a job was done poorly, that was the best way to get to do that service for another week.

+ Each child could have a pet as long as they managed the care and an agreed upon portion of the funding of the animal. Going outside twice a day to chore horses, goats, and pigs in the cold Indiana winters and hot Midwest summers developed commitment.

+ As a family we participated in regular devotions including Bible reading, Scripture memorization, and any discussion the reading triggered.

+ We rotated nights to prepare dinner. Little ones helped me in the kitchen.

+ While they were still at home, I helped each one start a checking and savings account, and manage their first credit card.

+ From college applications to invitations, 4-H forms to summer camp registrations to thank you notes, each teen filled out their own paperwork. I helped as needed.

Once a child proved their dependability at home by doing their chores and schoolwork without being told (aka, nagged), they earned the privilege to work outside the home.

My teens operated a family business as the *WELLSpring Fiddlers*. They traveled extensively, made recordings in Nashville, met talented professionals, and performed at a variety of venues. On a personal level it proved priceless as they worked together, divided responsibilities, managed money, learned to relate to all ages on a professional basis, and tithed on their income.

Observing my children as they grew up, I learned that teenagers have a fresh view of life and an intelligent wit. I recognized that kids and young adults alike respect authenticity. Truth, honest answers to their questions, and a genuine relationship with the Lord are priorities for teens.

I also learned that:

+ Letting each child have a voice in choosing their own activities helped ensure enthusiastic participation.
+ Listening to recorded books while driving ensured that even my reluctant readers received a wholesome diet of classics and excellent literature.
+ Some children, particularly my son, needed to learn from someone other than his mother. It was part of transitioning into a man.
+ Taking college courses while in high school gave them a jumpstart on their college requirements. One child earned a bachelor's degree at age twenty.

The best part of childhood is discovering, accepting, and celebrating a unique individuality. Growing up is a season of exploring and transitioning into adulthood. Developing children's strengths and encouraging each person's God-designed bent gives them the confidence to even fix Bach's music.

 If you are going to doubt something, doubt your limits.

Don Ward

◁ Look Back

Does your focus typically spotlight your strengths and the strengths of your children? Or do weaker areas garner the most attention?

▷ Move Ahead

Explore the interests of your children even though they may not be areas you ever considered. Encourage your children to follow their passion. Frequently parents insist that children devote themselves to areas that lead to a conventional job. Yet, our favorite books and movies are about those who dared to dream. The Happiest Place on Earth, Disneyland, was built because Walt Disney pursued his passion and we've enjoyed the benefits for generations. In the words of Cory Edwards, writer and producer of the feature film *Hoodwinked*, "Do what you love and the money will follow."

> To succeed in life, you need three things:
> a wishbone, a backbone, and a funny bone.
>
> REBA MCENTIRE

CHAPTER 15

BEFORE THE CLOCK STRIKES TWELVE

Am I savoring the splendid moments?

Seek freedom and become captive of your desires,
seek discipline and find your liberty.

FRANK HERBERT

Lord, could I please have a black Lab puppy and a set of drums?"
Nightly it was my son's faithful prayer. Though I didn't say anything, the *last* item on my prayer list was a black Labrador puppy and a set of drums. For months my nine-year-old boy faithfully prayed.

One day at a nearby farm with a sign out front that read "Free Puppies," a Lab pup broke from the litter and ran forward to choose my son. "Mama," Josiah asked, "if I eat all my vegetables and clean my room, can I keep this puppy?"

"Look, son," I outlined, "are you going to train this dog so it's a good, obedient dog?"

"I will," Josiah promised.

"And clean up the dog flops?"

"I'll clean up after the dog," Josiah solemnly assured.

"If you bring home this dog it will be your dog. Is that a deal?"

"Yes, Mama, I'll take care of the dog."

Josiah named the pup Old Dan after the male puppy in the book *Where the Red Fern Grows.*

The following weekend, I went garage sale-ing. It was Josiah's turn to have some alone time with me so he scratched Old Dan behind his floppy ears, jumped into the passenger seat and away we went. At the first garage sale we came to, what did we find but a complete set of drums all assembled and ready to play. I looked at Josiah. Josiah looked at me.

I grinned. What's a mom to do?

A week later he was playing those garage sale drums in a fiddle show.

Under Josiah's training, Old Dan went on to become the 4-H grand champion dog in obedience. I grew fond of the free, mixed breed answer to prayer. Old Dan plays with the children, minds his manners for the most part, barks when someone arrives, and he talks. Dan has a singsong way of whining. It's nice to have a verbal male around the house.

Neither the drums nor the dog were on my prayer list but they were on Josiah's. My son learned that all good things come to those who pray and go to garage sales. His childhood is highlighted by his two loves—his drums and his dog.

After a year in the military, my son came home for Thanksgiving weekend. We were thrilled to embrace him and there was something poignant about a ten-year-old dog named Dan who saw this man and recognized his boy.

 We are what we repeatedly do. Excellence, then, is not an act, but a habit.

Aristotle

Nurturing families requires *time,* a precious commodity in our fast-paced culture. We must purposely take the time to love and connect with our families in creative and unique ways. My friend calls this being a purposeful parent.

Here lies the key to family life. Rather than apples and oranges, our individual families are pineapples and kumquats. The most courageous parents do what is best for their child no matter what anybody else thinks. Or what we think they think. Outward impressions are meaningless and when we are doing what God has put in our hands to do—parent our children—we're not concerned about what others may or may not think about us. God looks at our hearts. Our family members do the same.

Our job description as a parent is to know our child. We have the rare privilege of understanding the individuality and natural bent of each unique child and encouraging his growth and spirituality from that perspective. While there are universal principles of respect and honor, what works for one family or child can be creatively different from what is successful for another. When one of my children is affectionate, I know all is well with her world. When another is clingy, it is a sign that she is feeling insecure.

We tailor our acts of nurturing to each child. Children flourish with clarity. They like to know exactly what is expected. Each birthday, my friend gives her children one privilege and one responsibility. These are carefully outlined in writing so if there is any confusion, parent and child can go back to the agreement and come to an understanding, sometimes adding additional wording.

When my children became adults and still lived at home, we put together an agreement that looked something like this:

> Congratulations! You are an amazing young man/woman, and you and I recognize that you are an adult.
>
> You already manage your own schedule, your finances, your dog, and your car.

House rules include:
>   Daily do your service (chore).
>   Help with yard work in a timely manner.
>   Use only your own computer settings on the family computer. Log off the Internet when you are done.
>   Clean up after yourself regarding dishes, laundry, bathroom, etc.
>   Be respectful of your roommates—me and your siblings.

As an adult, scheduling your doctor and dental visits are your responsibility. Our insurance will cover those items as well as your prescriptions and you will pay the co-pays.

Clothing, personal items, and gas are your responsibility.

I will provide an awesome place to live staffed with your adoring fan club, food, shampoo, toilet paper, and laundry soap.

Much love,
Mama

Interestingly, my children reflect much of me. Too much, if you ask me. If I do not have discipline, I can't expect my children to. If I am not passionate in my life, I won't see passion in theirs. When I'm sloppy with my finances and health, this will show up in my children.

That's reality. Do I always like it? Hardly. Especially when what I see reflected back reminds me that I'm being slippery in some aspect of my life. Being a parent is a grand adventure, a universal privilege, and a gigantic responsibility. If I want my children to walk in liberty and relationship with the Lord, I must first do it myself. Then I can support them in their own journey.

When it comes to battlegrounds, I've learned from wiser parents who parented before me to choose character over appearance. One close friend in church leadership graciously received raised eyebrows and stage whispers from her peers because of her teens' appearance. One child sported purple hair, another wore long hair when it wasn't fashionable for boys, and a third was the first on their block and in their congregation to have piercings.

Perhaps not mainstream with the norm, these three young people learned a lot about the people in the church and about personal faith. Their journey merely looked different from the others who conformed to unwritten rules about what kids who attend church should look like.

Particularly with current trends, there is a lot of leeway for me and my children to be fashionably unique. I encourage their creativity in fashion while stressing modesty. This protects reputations in addition to being a matter of safety.

I am grateful for the loving mentors who have come alongside and invested in my children. Frequently someone will connect specially with just one child, recognizing their strengths. Since, as one friend reminds me, I have a litter of children, I rejoice when those kindred spirit interactions occur.

The children have quickly come to celebrate these relationships for each other as well. Each of us is a vital, irreplaceable part of our family and each of us is an individual who enjoys being noticed and appreciated. There have been coaches, art teachers, music instructors, and friends who have developed a one-on-one friendship with different members of my family. I'm thankful that they are on my team.

 He has all the virtues I dislike and none of the vices I admire.

Winston Churchill

◁ Look Back

What are the unique characteristics of each of your children? Are there unimportant areas where you have invested too much negative energy? Someone once observed that often what a child got in trouble for as a youngster is what they get paid to do as an adult.

▷ Move Ahead

Take it from a mom who has several adult children. Even though we have our young with us longer than any other mothers on the planet, our babies grow up and get their own life all too soon. We only have eighteen summers together. Only eighteen Christmases. Eighteen birthdays. What purposeful ways will you initiate today to regularly enjoy the priceless moments you have with your children? How can you focus on their strengths and celebrate their unique characteristics?

> You cannot bring up boys as eagles
> and expect them to turn out sparrows.
>
> MRS. ROOSEVELT, SPEAKING ABOUT HER FIGHTER PILOT SON
> DOWNED IN COMBAT IN *THE ERA OF THEODORE ROOSEVELT*
> BY GEORGE E. MOWRY

CHAPTER 16

HEIGH-HO, HEIGH-HO

Does the to-do list ever end?

I arise in the morning torn between a desire to
improve the world and a desire to enjoy the world.
That makes it hard to plan the day.

E. B. WHITE

My brain knows this is the right decision; my heart feels
sorry for him. As for me, I have slept and slept and
slept. People tell me that I look rested—what a wonder.
Today, for the first time in months I woke up without a
stomachache or pain in my shoulders. This has been a
living death. Do we ever get over missing being in love?
Wanting what it could have been? No. We adjust. My
goal is to eat better, learn who I am again—surely more
than ex-wife and mom and caretaker. Let the fragments
grow that were neglected while I was trying to save my
dying marriage. I'd like to go away and be alone for a
while—but I'm already alone. Every day, I try to do one
thing that is cleaning up my life (house or yard), and tell
myself it is okay to lie in bed or just watch TV.

NEWLY SINGLE

Have you seen the runaway alarm clock? Emitting a random pattern of beeps and flashes, this personable alarm clock rolls away and hides when I hit the snooze button. Battery operated, made from shatter-resistant materials, and mounted on two rubber wheels, it bounces down from the nightstand, navigating over wood or carpet floors to wedge deep into corners so I have to get up, seek it out, and slap it silly. I mean shut it off. This is the ultimate wake-up call for those of us who would prefer to get up at the crack of noon.

Some days I can't wait to get up. Other days I'd rather hide under the covers until reality goes away.

After raising five children on her own and managing three businesses, my friend and mentor suggested I title this book, *What To Do When You're Doing It Alone*. "Face it," Saundra told me, "if anything's gonna get done, it's because we do it."

Like the psalmist, I say, "I lift up my eyes to the hills—where does my help come from?" (Ps. 121:1).

When I feel like I don't have time to take on another project, I devote just 15 minutes per day to that item. At the end of five days, I have invested over an hour in progress on that goal.

 I am only one, but still I am one. I cannot do everything, but still I can do something. And because I cannot do everything, I will not refuse to do the something that I can do.

Edward Everett Hale

Most writers must hold down a day job. These passionate or zany people don't have the time they wish to write but it is common for a writer to get up early or stay up an extra hour to devote themselves to their craft. At the end of a week, a writer who spends an hour per day at the keyboard has seven hours of work completed. Successful writers such as Jerry Jenkins, author of the Left Behind series and a hundred other books, and top literary agent Chip MacGregor both admit they probably got more consistent writing done when they had to carve an hour from the front or end of the day while maintaining a regular nine-to-five job. I wrote my first book between the hours of 10:00 PM and 1:00 AM.

I'm learning to keep my eye on the prize. What do I most want to accomplish? Then, each day I set a doable goal around that focus and do that task first. If I must make a phone call, I make that call prior to making other calls.

Becoming the head of my household meant I had to give myself permission to value my time and my worth. When I was married, I served as support to my husband. I gave my time and effort to support his work, his goals, and his schedule. It took me years to realize I could, indeed *had* to give myself the same importance. Until I did, I made no significant progress financially or career-wise because I continued to put everyone else's projects before my own.

Focus and commitment are the secrets of productive people. Successful people target the important above the urgent and give that precedence over the other emergencies that clamor for our time and attention.

Before going to bed, one friend lists three priorities for the following day. She does those items first and consistently makes measurable progress on her goals. At the start of each week, she maps out what is important for that week including rest and playtime with her children. Each month and each year, she schedules the priority events on the calendar.

When asked to do something, another friend always responds, "I'll pray about it and get back to you." What a good idea. She has a policy of praying and waiting at least twenty-four hours before taking on a new obligation. Surprisingly, there have been significant instances when she was positive she would not accept a responsibility but during prayer God impressed on her that she was exactly the right person for the project.

There is no benefit to being rigid or controlled by a calendar. But there is freedom in planning ahead for important dates balanced by adequate rest. This protects our schedule from becoming a burden that steals our peace. We safeguard our time with our children. We protect our financial and career goals. We know when saying yes aligns with our lifestyle and when to say no.

By scheduling time for work, children, managing finances, home maintenance, and social engagements, we shield ourselves from taking on more than we can fit in. Have you ever done that? Me neither.

It is tempting to dash hither and thither when pressures build. Being busy gives a false sense of importance. Instead, carving moments to schedule and plan pays valuable dividends toward my goals. Keeping my priority list in sight helps me evaluate what activities are essential to the values of my family and which ones may be good but are sidetracks.

Certainly there is more to do than I can get to. But I don't have to do it all at once. My priorities include:

Time connecting with the Lord

Mothering my children

Relationships before things

Consistent progress on my career

Regular attention to the finances and home maintenance

Many responsibilities are seasonal. Mowing and weeding, raking and shoveling. My friend who sews clothes for her children sets aside a week in the summer to stitch school clothes and a week before Christmas for making gifts. Women I know who bake, make enough on one day to last for the week. Several other women prepare and freeze a month's worth of favorite meals on one day, freeing up time daily for other demands. Paying bills on only one or two days per month keeps the finances simple. Grouping errands conserves time and effort.

It doesn't have to be hard. Embrace easy. When exhaustion dogs our heels, we serve up a cozy dinner of soup, sandwiches, and hot fudge sundaes by candlelight.

Accept offers of help. I made a rotating list of tasks I needed help with and then when someone asked, I had a ready answer. When friends dropped by, I quickly glanced at the list and asked for assistance with a lingering project. Develop systems that ease the schedules for others by offering to share carpooling responsibilities. For projects that are too big to tackle alone, build a Bible study or support group who assist each other.

 And why do you worry about clothes? See how the lilies of the field grow. They do not labor or spin. Yet I tell you that not even Solomon in all his splendor was dressed like one of these. If that is how God clothes the grass of the field, which is here today and tomorrow is thrown into the fire, will he not much more clothe you, O you of little faith? So do not worry, saying, "What shall we eat?" or "What shall we drink?" or "What shall we wear?" For the pagans run after all these things, and your heavenly Father knows that you need them. But seek first his kingdom and his righteousness, and all these things will be given to you as well.

Matthew 6:28–33

Decluttering is the secret ingredient of a peaceful home. Ongoing decluttering reduces maintenance and guarantees I have less to weed through when searching for something. Less is more. Less is simpler. For me, the hardest part of decluttering is deciding what to keep and what to pass on. I am more effective when I'm angry, so that's a positive way to channel my emotions. Ironically, after I give something away or sell it, I think about how I could use it now. Maybe there's medication for that.

Hoarding is bondage. It is difficult to live life when we have to wade through piles of stuff. Since most of it is never used, the stuff goes to ruin while we are tripping over it.

After years of barely having enough to get by, my friend saved everything. As she grew to trust the Lord to provide for her and to trust herself to make good decisions, she dove into decluttering the stacks of stuff she had sought security in. "The stuff in my shed had all decomposed," she reported. "I was embarrassed when I took a trailerful to the dump."

At its core, hoarding is idolatry. It is holding on to things out of fear and trusting in my ability to provide for myself rather than trusting in God as my source, my protector, and my provision. Certainly it is wise to stock up on basic necessities. This is recommended as a precaution for any emergency from terrorism to natural disasters to a sudden influx of relatives or a teenager with friends in tow. Friends who found themselves unemployed for months at a time were thankful for a well-stocked pantry and the six months of income they had banked.

We declutter our living spaces by putting those hoarded possessions back into circulation. Have a garage sale, put it on eBay, or donate to a local charity.

Serenity is found in simple, clean living spaces for you and your family. The world can be cruel and chaotic. As makers of the home, we have the ability to create an environment free of unkind words. Free of harsh noises. With a comfortable calendar, organized living spaces, and gentle words, our homes become a haven. A haven where our family returns for rest and refreshment. A welcoming place crafted by you.

 Where there is room in the heart there is room in the home.

Needlepoint wisdom

◁ Look Back

What tasks around the home can you do yourself? What tasks can the children help with? What tasks do you need help with?

▷ Move Ahead

From the list of items you need help with, create a plan to ask for assistance, trade skills with someone who can do this, or make a plan to pay for the service.

> I am always doing that which I can not do,
> in order that I may learn how to do it.
>
> PABLO PICASSO

CHAPTER 17

No More Damsel in Distress

Where do I find courage?

Courage is doing what you're afraid to do.
There can be no courage unless you're scared.
EDDIE RICKENBACKER

On a balmy Midwest evening, I sat at an aged high school desk in an airplane hangar and signed the seemingly one-hundredth paper promising neither I nor my remaining relatives would sue in the event I wound up on the ground in a form resembling a cow patty.

I glanced up at the slender man my age, puffing down another cigarette. "Lost anyone yet?"

"Not a one."

"How many jumps have you made?"

"Seventeen hundred."

I signed the final paper and handed him the stack.

Eyeing my build, the smoker pulled a jumpsuit from the selection on the rack. I wriggled into it while nearby a shirtless guy with gray chest hair expertly packed parachutes. Outside the hangar door, dressed in shorts, flip flops, and a Hawaiian shirt, another guy paced while he talked on a cell phone.

Crushing out his cigarette, my jump partner popped a mint into his mouth and checked my suit. "You're good to go." He pointed to the waiting airplane.

A former two-seater, the passenger seat had been removed and the interior stripped to allow space for jumpers. No longer on his cell phone, our pilot climbed in and strapped on his seatbelt.

Settled inside with my back against the pilot's seat, I traced the Navy SEAL emblem on the window. "Which team were you on?"

The pilot navigated the small plane down the runway. "SEAL team five."

While the plane corkscrewed up into the expansive sky, my jump partner explained the sequence for getting out of the plane at ten thousand feet. "We'll free-fall for five thousand feet," he said. "Then I'll pull the parachute cord and we'll glide down for the last half and do a perfect landing at the airport field."

Above the engine's roar, I gave the okay sign.

"You think you've flown before? No way." He glanced at the pilot who nodded. "What you are about to do is really flying."

Minutes later the pilot straightened our course and announced we were at jump level. My jump partner opened the plane door. I scooted to the opening, stood up, and reached outside to grasp the wing while I stepped outside onto the footstep. Crossing my arms across my chest, I grinned at the pilot and lifted my feet. The airplane flew out from under me. It was awesome.

Faith is stepping into life because I trust God. Trust is faith in action. I may believe a parachute can glide me to earth from ten thousand feet but I exercise trust when I smile at the pilot and jump out of a perfectly good airplane. At that moment, the wind took my breath like I was a pup in the back of a speeding pickup truck. Marveling at the bird's-eye view of the horizon and the beauty of the landscape below, I placed my trust and whole life into the object of my faith.

Trust and courage are partners. Best friends forever, attached at the hip, Siamese twins. They come and go together.

Throughout Scripture, God is referred to by many names. Each name is descriptive of our Heavenly Father's character. Each name tells us something important about our mighty and trustworthy God.

Elohim: The Creator
El Elyon: The God Most High
El Roi: The God Who Sees
El Shaddai: The All-Sufficient One
Adonai: The Lord
Jehovah: The Self-Existent One
Johovah-jireh: The Lord Will Provide
Jehovah-rapha: The Lord Who Heals
Jehovah-nissi: The Lord My Banner
Jehovah-mekoddishkem: The Lord Who Sanctifies You
Jehovah-shalom: The Lord Is Peace
Jehovah-sabaoth: The Lord of Hosts
Jehovah-raah: The Lord My Shepherd
Jehovah-tsidkenu: The Lord Our Righteousness
Jehovah-shammah: The Lord Is There

When I looked at my situation it appeared much bigger than me. Courage came when I concentrated on God who is mightier than my circumstances. Perspective depends on where I put my focus. When I understand something about the steadfastness and trustworthiness of God's character it is easier for me trust him in times of change.

The call to follow our Lord is a call to courage. It is often a call to change. For nearly everyone in the Bible, God's call impacted career, culture, identity, family, or reputation. God's call changes geography, civilization, and the course of history. The disciples stopped fishing and carried the good news to the world. David abandoned shepherding and became the father of kings. Moses quit herding sheep and led a nation to freedom. Mary and Joseph traveled away from their hometown and nurtured God's only son.

For you and me the call to courage is a call to change. Our marital status changed. Our social status changed. Our finances changed, maybe for the better. Our schedule changed. Our dreams changed. Our address may have changed. Our emotions, family dynamics, friends, insurance, possessions . . .

We can think we are trusting God when we say, "I am trusting God that he won't let [fill in the blank with your pet concern] happen to me." But true trust comes when the thing we most dread does happen and we are able to trust God in the midst of it and survive with our faith intact.

Change. We can embrace it or resist it. What we resist persists. At the foundation of much of our fear, we are reluctant to embrace God's direction because we resist the change it may bring to our lives. It certainly meant I had to venture into the unknown. Some days that was exciting. Other days I would prefer to remain shallow. We get comfortable surrounded by what we know and what is familiar. Change required more effort as I learned to live in new surroundings, with different routines, unusual experiences, and fresh relationships. It meant venturing into places and situations I am not accustomed to. Some intrepid souls thrive on adventure but most of us are content to be homebodies.

 Even if you think you're on the right track, you'll get run over if you just sit there.

Will Rogers

Queen Esther was called to courage. Her status changed from Mordecai's niece to the young and lovely bride of the unpredictable and powerful King Xerxes. Cautioned to keep her Hebrew heritage a secret, she found herself the sole protector of her people from genocide.

"And who knows but that you have come to royal position for such a time as this?" (Esther 4:14).

To you, I say the same: Who knows but that you have been placed in this situation for such a time as this? Like Esther, we can use this opportunity, this crossroad in our life, with nobility.

Deborah faced a similar challenge. Her country went to war against a sadistic enemy. Focusing on the enemy, the general of the Hebrew army agreed to face the enemy only if Deborah went with him. Focusing on God, Deborah was not intimidated by the deadly foe but donned courage and off to war she went.

> Show me a sign for good, that those who hate me may see it and be ashamed, because You, LORD, have helped me and comforted me.
>
> Psalm 86:17 NKJV

When King Saul and his army were arrayed against the Philistines, the entire Hebrew army trembled at the daily challenge to do battle with the Philistine champion, Goliath. Dressed in state-of-the-art armor and standing nine feet and nine inches tall, he was an imposing menace. Every morning and night for forty days, the giant harassed them, "This day I defy the ranks of Israel! Give me a man and let us fight each other" (1 Sam. 17:10).

The Israelites saw the giant and thought he was too big. With his focus set on God, David saw Goliath and figured he was too big to miss.

God invites us into his family. "Yet to all who received him, to those who believed in his name, he gave the right to become children of God—children born not of natural descent, nor of human decision or a husband's will, but born of God" (John 1:12–13).

In this place of belonging, God invites us to partner with him. "Come and see," Jesus said to his disciples (John 1:39 NKJV).

"Follow me," Jesus said (Matt. 4:19). After his resurrection, Jesus met with the disciples on the shore of their beloved Sea of Galilee. Over a satisfying meal of grilled fish, Jesus reiterated to Peter, "You follow Me!" (John 21:22 NASB).

His last commandment was given moments before his ascension to Heaven: "Therefore go and make disciples of all nations, baptizing them in the name of the Father and of the Son and of the Holy Spirit, and teaching them to obey everything I have commanded you. And surely I am with you always, to the very end of the age" (Matt. 28:19–20). Go and tell.

 When thought becomes excessively painful, action is the finest remedy.

Salman Rushdie

Come and see. Follow me. Go and tell. Instead of concentrating on the thou-shalt-nots of do not steal, do not lie, and do not commit murder, we can enjoy doing the dos. Courage is about doing. The dos are a lot more fun.

- "Love the Lord your God with all your heart and with all your soul and with all your mind." (Matt. 22:37)
- "These commandments that I give you today are to be upon your hearts. Impress them on your children. Talk about them when you sit at home and when you walk along the road, when you lie down and when you get up." (Deut. 6:6–7)
- "Love your neighbor as yourself." (Matt. 22:39)
- "Follow me." (Matt. 4:19)

Go and tell. Noah took up shipbuilding and witnessed the complete change of the entire world. Abraham changed his address. Jonah journeyed to Nineveh. Paul changed his name and his trade. Each one knew the Lord (come and see), had a relationship with God (follow me), and received instruction regarding where they were to go and what they were to do (go and tell).

Joseph, Mary's husband in the New Testament, was a picture of obedience to the voice of God. "Because Joseph her husband was a righteous man and did not want to expose her to public disgrace, he had in mind to divorce her quietly. But after he had considered this, an angel of the Lord appeared to him in a dream and said, 'Joseph son of David, do not be afraid to take Mary home as your wife, because what is conceived in her is from the Holy Spirit. She will give birth to a son, and you are to give him the name Jesus, because he will save his people from their sins.' . . . When Joseph woke up, he did what the angel of the Lord had commanded him and took Mary home as his wife" (Matt. 1:19–21, 24).

Joseph responded immediately to God's next command. "An angel of the Lord appeared to Joseph in a dream. 'Get up,' he said, 'take the child and his mother and escape to Egypt. Stay there until I tell you, for Herod is going to search for the child to kill him.' So he got up, took the child and his mother during the night and left for Egypt" (Matt. 2:13–14).

Joseph's instant obedience left no quarter for fear to halt or hinder him. His immediate action positively impacted his circle of influence that, centuries later, includes you and me.

Does God honor delayed obedience? Jonah is the visual aid for that. When God called Jonah to travel to the sinful city of Nineveh and call the Ninevites to repentance, Jonah booked a ticket on the first boat bound in the opposite direction. All-seeing God sent a great storm and the sailors drew lots to find out who had attracted this disaster. For Jonah, the short end of the stick meant a quick drop into the drink. Unlike Jonah, a hefty fish was instantly obedient to God and swallowed Jonah. Whole. In the belly of the fish, Jonah prayed for three days until he and God reached an understanding.

Conveniently, the fish vomited Jonah onto Nineveh's shore. Bleached white by his stomach-acid bath, Jonah made quite an impression when he entered the city and proclaimed God's message. Though delayed, Jonah's obedience resulted in the entire city's repentance.

Of the two, instant obedience rather than delayed obedience was easier on the follower. I can choose to make my life easier.

It takes courage to let go of control. Only to find I was never really in complete control anyway. Frequently, controllers have experienced deep hurt or betrayal or both. They respond by striving to control situations, environments, and people in a desperate attempt to protect themselves from being hurt or betrayed again.

Adam and Eve tried to control their surroundings after eating the forbidden fruit. They made coverings from fig leaves to cloak their nakedness and hid when God came to walk with them as he customarily did in the cool of the evening. We hear the grief in God's voice as he calls to Adam, "Where are you?"

"I heard you in the garden," Adam answered, "and I was afraid because I was naked; so I hid" (Gen. 3:10).

Following their life and history-changing disobedience, they ran from God. How often do you and I run from God rather than run to him? Dodge the relationship with the very one whose perfect love for you and me casts out fear?

Trust, the absence of fear, is essential to an intimate relationship with God. "As the Father has loved me, so have I loved you. Now remain in my love. If you obey my commands, you will remain in my love, just as I have obeyed my Father's commands and remain in his love. I have told you this so that my joy may be in you and that your joy may be complete. My command is this: Love each other as I have loved you. Greater love has no one than this, that he lay down his life for his friends. You are my friends if you do what I command" (John 15:9–14).

"How do you know that our beliefs are the right ones?" My children have each questioned which religion is truth since all claim to be the true faith. Such questioning is healthy and the search for answers is the journey that ends in each of us making our relationship with Christ genuine.

Foundational for Christ-followers is that Christ loved us first. He sought us out and paid the penalty for your sin and mine when he died on the cross. No other so-called deity comes to us in love, requiring nothing more than that we accept his gift of grace, forgiveness, and eternal life together. Further evidence of Christ's Lordship is that his tomb is empty. He rose from the dead, proving his sovereignty over our most powerful enemy of death. The gift of the daily presence of his Holy Spirit is the gift of relationship now. There is no waiting.

The Lord does not ask from us anything that he does not first give. He exercised unforgettable courage in leaving the comfort and position of eternal heaven to enter time as the earthly Jesus. Living a sinless life for thirty-three years in the midst of family feuding and ridicule, under Roman oppression, and as a single, he then poured out his life for you and me on the cross at Calvary.

God loves us perfectly and understands, which is why we go to him for the source of our courage. Loving God gives me the courage to come and see, follow, and go and tell. His perfect love equips me to trust him when he beckons me to change.

I have learned these truths about courage and about the love of God:
1. I don't have to be perfect.
2. I don't have to be strong all the time.
3. What I used to call mistakes are actually valuable learning experiences and prove I'm in the game.

"My grace is sufficient for you, for my power is made perfect in weakness" (2 Cor. 12:9). In my weakness, he is strong.

When I'm fearful, running to God rather than away opens the door to adventure. Sometimes I crave adventure. Other times I resist God's call because I am afraid of what the next step may be. It may be out of my comfort zone. Like Abraham, Daniel, and Joseph, it may mean relocation. Like Deborah, Esther, and Gideon, it may mean leadership. As it did for Moses, Peter, John, and Paul, it could mean a shift in employment. A common first reaction to what we don't know or understand is either excitement or fear. Too often I choose fear. Choosing excitement is a lot more fun and fulfilling.

I may fear the unknown but there is no unknown to God.

◁ Look Back

What does courage look like for you? When have you resisted beneficial changes in your life?

▷ Move Ahead

Lean on the Lord as you follow his lead to "Come and see," "Follow me," and "Go and tell." What change can you embrace with enthusiasm?

Anyone God uses significantly is
always deeply wounded.

BRENNAN MANNING

CHAPTER 18

BEYOND THE WISHING WELL

Am I significant?

No believer should let fear of failure
prevent them from responding fully to the call of God.
Everything needed for life and godliness has been
provided and is immediately at work in every
believer that obeys God's call.

HENRY BLACKABY

During World War I, the commander of the 91st British Infantry Brigade required the brigade to daily repeat Psalm 91. When all other infantry claimed only a 10 percent survival rate, Col. Whittlesey's entire 91st Brigade survived four years of battle. These men placed their faith in God, trusted his promised Word, and went forward in courage.

Amy Carmichael brought life and belonging to the children she welcomed to her orphanage and later led to safety. It took courage for Margaret Thatcher to be England's prime minister. Amelia Earhart modeled courage as a female pilot. It took courage for Margaret Ringenberg to be one of America's first female air force pilots during

World War II. Ringenberg was still flying air races well into her eighties. And winning.

Whether she was being honored at the prestigious Gathering of Eagles or was one of President Bush's invited guests for the dedication of the Air Force Memorial in Washington, D.C., Ringenberg would board a commercial flight and poke her head into the cockpit.

"I've flown longer than any of you have," she would remind the pilot and copilot.

That's well earned spunk.

I long to live a life of significance. When all is said and done, I would like the history books to note that I made a difference in the world. And on this side of divorce, I wonder if it is too late for me. Did I miss my chance?

"This is what the Lord Almighty says: 'Give careful thought to your ways. Go up into the mountains and bring down timber and build the house, so that I may take pleasure in it and be honored,' says the Lord" (Hag. 1:7–8). God called Haggai when he was eighty years old to assemble the people and rebuild the temple of the Lord.

Grandma Moses began painting in her eighties. Dr. Marvin Baker was in his eighties when he developed the international teen writing and art competition that launched careers and provided a dozen college scholarships to talented teenagers. Age doesn't matter. A life lived doing anything other than what God calls us to do is a dissatisfied life but we can answer God's call to significance at any age and at any place.

We know when we are following Christ. The evidence is that we bear fruit. "This is to my Father's glory, that you bear much fruit, showing yourselves to be my disciples" (John 15:8). "But the fruit of the Spirit is love, joy, peace, patience, kindness, goodness, faithfulness, gentleness and self-control" (Gal. 5:22–23).

A lack of faith and courage leads to an ungrateful heart and that leads to disobedience. Selfishness is the antithesis of trust. When I notice myself grumbling and my conversation centers around complaints instead of appreciation, it is the fruit of ungratefulness. I can trace that back to a lack of faith and choosing fear over courage.

 Better to do something imperfectly than to do nothing flawlessly.

Robert Schuller

Looking Glass: Is my life characterized by love, joy, peace, patience, kindness, goodness, faithfulness, gentleness, and self-control?

Is my conversation centered on negativity and complaining?

Am I being selfish?

When I am complaining and striving over some issue that has my underwear all in a wad, it is to my benefit to stop in the midst of my whining and consider: five years from now will I look back and think this was worth the negative energy and emotion I am expending on it?

 It is not length of life, but depth of life.

Ralph Waldo Emerson

Saying thank you is powerful. Saying thank you frequently is one way I can quickly and easily make the world a better place. Beyond expressing thanks to those in my circle of influence, I have plenty to thank the Lord for.

I made a list. I'm thankful for my
children
home
talents
friends
income
health
laptop
promising future

Thanksgiving is an ideal time to set out a basket with blank paper and pens. Throughout the season, family and guests scribble their thank yous to the Lord and the basket quickly fills. On a wall we tape up a tree trunk made of brown construction paper. Family and guests write their thank yous on green construction paper leaves and tape the leaves to the tree. By the end of the season, we have a fully leafed out tree declaring the works of the Lord in our lives.

One dinner tradition is to go around the table and each person states something they are thankful for. On birthdays and special occasions, we each say something about the guest of honor that we are thankful for.

The Broadway story *Mame* gave us the lyric, "We need a little Christmas, right this very minute." I propose we give thanks a minimum of once a day rather than merely once a year. Thankfulness is a trust thermometer. Would I trust God when conflict overshadowed my household?

You and I have experienced an overabundance of discord. My belief was that I could do something significant if I didn't have this invasive, sabotaging controversy tripping me up like shoestrings tied together.

When we come face-to-face with conflict, we are not alone. Everyone in the Old and New Testaments experienced opposition. Conflict is at the heart of every story. Consider the conflict that characterized the homes of Isaac, Jacob, Samuel, and David—men who were unquestionably called by God.

In the New Testament, the Holy Spirit led Jesus into the wilderness where he was tested by God and tempted by Satan. While all humans since Adam and Eve failed, Jesus passed the physical, spiritual, and psychological temptations. Deep in the heart of trials and temptation, Jesus responded with the heart of the matter—with Scripture.

When I'm tempted to allow fear to dictate my response to God's call, I can follow the strategy modeled by Christ and respond with God's Word. "And God is faithful; he will not let you be tempted beyond what you can bear. But when you are tempted, he will also provide a way out so that you can stand up under it" (1 Cor. 10:13). All the resources of the Father are mine including the power of his name, twenty-four-hour access to him, and a securely promised heritage. "I can do everything through him who gives me strength" (Phil. 4:13).

"These three remain: faith, hope and love. But the greatest of these is love" (1 Cor. 13:13). There will come a time when faith and hope are not necessary because there will just be love. God's perfect love. In the meantime, we put our faith into action through trust and our trust shows up in gratefulness and courage. We allow ourselves to be significant and embrace our passions in the midst of, and despite, the conflict that overshadows. Often it is friction that creates the context for you and me to walk and act with nobility.

At the crossroads of a marriage that has ended, the best thing is to get over it quickly. Make plans for the future and begin a new life with the children. They need something to move on *to*. So do you. It's the healthiest reaction and in the chaos and unspeakable pain, it's also the toughest.

 Courage is the greatest of all the virtues. Because if you haven't courage, you may not have an opportunity to use any of the others.

Samuel Johnson

It takes courage to venture forth, leaving the familiar behind. It's the only way to release another's hold and control over you, especially emotionally. The alternative is a constant tug of war—bickering, fighting, pulling, crying, and days of dark depression followed by nasty bitterness. Guess how I know. I'm the visual aid! Groveling, and hoping *this time* he'll change for the better is a formula for being abused. Confident people will come out on top. If you're not confident, fake it till you make it.

◁ Look Back

When have you delayed your obedience to God? What were the consequences of that delay? When have you obeyed God's call? What did that feel like and what were the outcomes of that obedience, trust, and relationship with God?

▷ Move Ahead

Write down twenty-five things you are thankful for. In every situation, look for the positive. Regularly do something new or something out of your comfort zone.

> I determined never to stop until I had come to the end
> and achieved my purpose.
>
> DAVID LIVINGSTONE

CHAPTER 19

YELLOW BRICK ROAD

How do I get emotionally unstuck?

Action is the foundational key to all success.

PABLO PICASSO

Everything is either growing or decaying. Including you and me. Of the two options, I choose growth. I've seen the stuff that's been too long in my refrigerator.

Granted, after thirty sometimes it feels like patch, patch, patch to keep our bodies and lives in forward motion. My friend says she is in the snapdragon part of life. Part of her is snapped. The rest is draggin'. Some of us claim to be in the metallic years of life with silver in our hair, gold in our teeth, and lead in our butts. On days when you feel like that, I recommend you go parasailing, skydiving, scuba diving, or sign up for private pilot lessons. Really!

As a marriage relationship dies, it gets toxic. You've experienced decay firsthand. For me that was characterized by lots of things I couldn't do, opportunities I couldn't have, love that was withheld. Now it's time to shift into building and growth. To embrace freedom, choice, and fun.

Emotions for you and your children will continue to surface like the proverbial layers of an onion. Events, holidays, smells, songs, phone calls, memories, and visits will trigger old hurts and inflict new ones. The healing and the adapting process is not going to be over in the hoped for three months.

"Surely the intensity of the turmoil will dissipate," my friend consoled.

Nine years later I asked, "When did you say it would calm down? And stop calling me Shirley."

To facilitate healthy growth and achieve much-needed consistency for me and my children, I advocate self-expression.

I encourage freedom for my children to express feelings without inflicting additional hurt, and I make a conscious effort to create a safe environment for their feelings and emotions. Each family member feels different emotions at different times. One is optimistic while another is depressed and another is angry. In our situation, one would be on good terms with their father while another was in deep pain in the same relationship and another was feeling ostracized. While not always easy, we're getting better at allowing each person to be where they are in their journey.

The codicil to this rule is that it is not okay to use our feelings to hurt another. If I am angry, I cannot take out my anger on others. When I am depressed, it is not all right for me to drain the joy from those around me. When a child was hurt and angry, it was not acceptable to take out those emotions on the rest of us.

"You can say the same thing nicely," is a popular motto at our house. It means we welcome the honest expression of thoughts and feelings in a way that does not inflict pain on others. We don't have to agree with each other. Varied opinions are healthy. It is important to honor each family member's individuality and their freedom to feel differently about anything from the taste of lima beans and favorite movies, to how they feel about an estranged parent or having to attend an awkward family event.

"Never say anything that hurts another," my counselor advised.

My friend Denise taught me the value of encouraging relationships between my children and coaches, teachers, and Sunday school instructors. It helps to welcome good male role models into the family life and enroll sons in adventure experiences including Civil Air Patrol, sports, scouts, and hunting with friends.

Journaling was particularly useful for several of my children. Especially the ones that were not strong verbal communicators. I gave each of my young ones a blank book so they could write to me and I could write back. The understanding was that spelling and punctuation and grammar did not matter.

"Just write what you want, when you want, and put it next to my bed," I suggested. "I'll write back and put the book next to your bed."

There were periods when we wrote back and forth every day. There were times when the books lay forgotten on nightstands, collecting dust. Then one day, I would find a journal once more on my nightstand and open it to a page where a child had renewed a conversation, poured out their heart on paper in a way they could not do verbally, or had jotted down an observation. There might be a question. A rant. Often there was a quickly penned "I love you, Mama."

Just as often, those journals were a pleasant diversion where we conversed about holiday plans, Christmas lists, whispered hopes, and daring dreams.

It was helpful to provide outlets for creativity and expression through a variety of mediums from horseback riding to painting lessons to music instruction.

 In the beginner's mind there are many possibilities; in the expert's mind there are few.

Shunryu Suzuki

The children hung dream boards in their rooms. For one this was an oversized sheet of paper with career options written in bold colored markers. For others this looked like poster board with magazine photos glued on. One child pinned pictures of her goals onto a bulletin board.

"What do you want to do next? Where do you want to be in a year? What do you see yourself doing and being in five years?"

Yearly we let our dreams flow freely through pens onto pages of notebook paper. These sheets were rolled and tucked into an antique turquoise canning jar that faithfully held our scribblings while perched on a decorative shelf in the kitchen.

Halfway through the year we would see that we had accomplished several items pictured on the dream boards. Unrolling our ball jar writings a year later, we are always pleasantly surprised to find we've indeed accomplished things we were only dreaming about as we authored those pages.

 A pile of rocks ceases to be a pile of rocks when somebody contemplates it with the idea of a cathedral in mind.

Antoine de Saint-Exupéry

◁ Look Back

Dream big. What does each family member dream of one day being or doing? What are your dreams?

▷ Move Ahead

Create a dream board for each family member and post them where they can easily be seen. Encourage each child to be involved in an outside activity that develops their abilities and connects them to positive people. Choose an activity for yourself, as well.

Doubt yourself and you doubt everything you see.
Judge yourself and you see judges everywhere.

But if you listen to the sound of your own voice,
you can rise above doubt and judgment.
And you can see forever.

NANCY KERRIGAN

CHAPTER 20

A Goose That Lays Golden Eggs

Is financial freedom possible?

I don't like money, actually,
but it quiets my nerves.

JOE LOUIS

God will not leave you hanging alone," my friend wrote in a letter. "He will provide for your every need. With only a thousand dollars per month, I have lived this for years. God has always provided better than had I controlled it myself. I know it is easier said than done but let go of your plan and wait on his plan. You have the tenacity, intelligence, and perseverance to pull this off. You can do this, my friend."

As an English major who never found x and declares math to be a four-letter word, if I can tackle my finances, even embrace them, you can too.

We can enjoy abundance in the midst of this new beginning. There are strategies to survive today and prepare for the future. Many women have grown up to believe that a man is our financial plan. But what if we never marry? What if the husband we are counting on is not financially savvy? What if our marriage ends?

The state I lived in at the time of my divorce held the uncoveted top spot in the nation for bankruptcy and foreclosure. A corollary was that it held a similar rating for divorce. The two are doubtless connected. People who are not mindful of their marriages will not be mindful of their finances and vice versa.

Whether married or single, my financial health, like my physical and emotional health, is my responsibility. While I was financially responsible for myself prior to marriage, after marriage the finances were completely controlled by my husband. The phones, for instance, were in his name only. When I became single, I had a lot to learn about finances and I was overdue in taking responsibility for myself in this arena.

The transition from married to single, from financially supported to personally responsible, is rarely given forethought. One day the other side of the bed is vacant; overnight the money that was ours has become his. To the spouse moving on to something new, the financial pleas from those left behind are quickly tagged "desperation."

How would I fix the leak in the basement, and the garbage disposal that went on the fritz? Was there a mechanic I could trust? How would I save for retirement at this late stage in life? What about health insurance? The questions whirled in my mind like fruit in a blender.

My mentor had walked this journey years earlier. She recalled scrambling to work three jobs to feed and house her children. For many months she sent a check for my children. It was a lifeline of love and care when I felt alone, abandoned, and unlovable. She called every so often and let me cry and rage. She listened and affirmed that my feelings were normal in this situation. Then she gently reminded me that God is my source and that with him all things are *Him*possible.

Though she didn't live close, whenever we got together she bought us a meal or ice cream, something I could rarely do beyond the dollar menu. Once she took the children and me to a dollar store and told each of us we could spend a couple dollars on anything we wanted. The little girls selected toys, the big girls shopped for fragrant shampoos, and I chose large envelopes to mail submissions. It was a special treat.

That Christmas she invited us to meet her at a town midway between our addresses to see the Christmas lights and surprised us with a trip to a college apparel store where each of the children was given an amount to spend. Through her own painful experience, she taught me a lot about giving, saving, and spending.

Stepping into financial responsibility is a grand adventure.

To get started here are some basic first steps:

+ Establish a checking account.
+ Establish a savings account.
+ Establish an investment account.
+ Keep good records.

If possible, open your checking and savings at a credit union because the interest rates and perks are generally better than at a bank.

From your earnings give 10 percent to the Lord, 10 percent to your savings, and 10 percent to your investments. If you can't do that, begin with what you can. Start with 5 percent and work up. Even 1 percent is a good beginning. Always pay the Lord first in tithe as a thank you for his provision and recognition of his protection. This simple practice of giving and generosity is imperative to the natural law of sowing and reaping as well as the healthy balance of your spirit.

Pay yourself next. If you don't put money aside for yourself, there will not be any left at the end of the month. Paying yourself first is a strategy that allows you to save and budget the rest for living expenses. Millionaires pay themselves first. If it works for them, we can use that principle, too.

Always spend less than you earn. Put money aside each month to save and invest. As soon as you have enough, open a certificate of deposit, a mutual fund with a group such as Vanguard, or other investment account. You work for money. The goal is to get your money to work for you earning interest or dividends.

Regularly increase the amount you give, save, and invest. For decades I dreamed of taking my children to Hawaii on vacation. Each payday I put five or eight dollars into an account. I added money from side jobs and gifts and before long the dream became reality.

What is your dream? A car? A home? Education? Retirement?

 May the LORD make you increase, both you and your children. May you be blessed by the LORD, the Maker of heaven and earth.

Psalm 115:14–15

Taking control of my money and financial life was one of the greatest ways I became personally responsible. A book that clearly explained the basics and mapped out a five-month step-by-step program for me to systematically follow was Suze Orman's *Women and Money*. I read through the book on my own and then asked a couple of ladies to go through it with me. Weekly we held each other accountable to read a chapter and work through the steps.

Next, I got a copy for each of my adult daughters so we could go through the book together. For each step in the book's five-step process toward putting their financial life in order that my daughters accomplished, I offered to deposit fifty dollars into their bank accounts.

Whether you check out that book from the library or find another financial intelligence program to follow, don't hesitate to get support for this part of your life, particularly if this is not an area where you are well versed. You truly cannot afford to be ignorant or ill prepared to handle your finances.

Money is the commodity that defines much of our quality of life in addition to the level of peace and generosity we enjoy. Establish a plan so you know how much money you have coming in and what expenses are going out and on what days they must be paid. Though it may be tempting to justify that we'll get to it later, it is vital to open our bills on the day they arrive. We give ourselves the gift of peace of mind when we pay bills early.

Keep accurate records in your checking register or on your computer so you know at all times what you have in your accounts. When you charge something, immediately deduct that amount from your checking. When you make a deposit, add it. When you write checks, subtract that number. Immediately. Daily know what you have in your accounts. It is easy.

Carry a one hundred dollar bill in the back of your wallet. It is good for your confidence and is there in case of emergency. See how long you can carry it there. Like motivational speaker Bob Harrison says, if you've been keeping company with Abraham Lincolns in the form of one dollar bills in your wallet, make new friends with Ben Franklins in the form of one hundred dollar bills. They are a good crowd to get used to associating with.

Honor yourself by respecting your worth. Do you regularly put yourself on sale? Make as much money as you can. To make less is selfish. The more you have, the more you have to give. When I have an abundance of money, I can fund excellent programs. The more money I have, the more I can contribute to support ministries, causes, and invest in people. Having a lot of money to be generous with is a great way to make a difference in the world.

If you are the sole provider for your children or anyone else, make sure your life insurance coverage will provide for them in case something happens to you.

 In times of profound change, the learners inherit the earth, while the learned find themselves beautifully equipped to deal with a world that no longer exists.

Eric Hoffer

Considering finances, we build backward. I make a list of what I want my lifestyle to be. I desire to take my family on vacations and make wise and lucrative investments so that my children don't have to take care of me in my old age. That means I want regular income. Toward that end, I plan for submitting marketable topics to the right publications. Creating this business plan requires prayer, time, and some good old-fashioned hard work. I seek wise counsel from others who have successfully established a successful financial plan.

Is there value to counting pennies? Relocating? Cutting coupons? My friend Denise is the coupon queen. She is the lady who buys $100 worth of groceries for $9.99. Sometimes I think the stores pay her to take her groceries home. Not one to have extra funds to give, she is the first to stock someone's pantry or bring a meal. She also uses coupons to take her children to hotels with a pool and breakfast in large cities for mini-vacations. For her, coupons are a fast track to multiplying her limited income. She researches scholarship programs for herself and her children in their areas of interest from sports to 4-H to college. She and her amazing children are exactly who philanthropic organizations had in mind when they established these opportunities.

Denise sold her home and purchased one that she could better maintain and afford in a nice neighborhood near the children's schools. Her family appreciated the new address that was free from negative memories. It was fresh for creating the next chapter of their collective life.

After nine years of keeping my beautiful six-acre Indiana gentleman's farm, I sold it when my divorce was final and relocated to a place that was allergen free for my youngest. It was time for my beloved home to fulfill someone else's dream while we moved on to new dreams.

Initially I chose to stay during the long separation to provide a sense of security for the children while their parents' marriage was in convulsions. By the time we moved, I was exhausted from single-handedly maintaining the lovely acreage. A lot of that was my determination to prove I could do this, and I did. But it didn't have to be that hard. Interestingly, one of my children wanted to relocate from the beginning of the separation to leave behind poor memories and create new ones.

My neighbor Lucille saved pennies to buy Christmas gifts each year. Counting pennies is beneficial but having to tightly watch finances can also be exhausting. My goal is that women create lifestyles that enable them to live joyfully without money being a dictator or source of bondage.

There is freedom in living in a budget. Knowing what I have to spend and staying in that amount allows me to put aside money, invest, and not be stressed about creditors. Going into debt, particularly with credit cards, mortgages my future and prohibits me from going and doing grand adventures today and tomorrow.

It is vital that we build into our lives spaces to loosen up. We are avid library users. We check out lots of resources from DVDs to books to recorded books that we listen to in the car. These materials offer leisure and educational activities without taxing the finances.

Let your needs be known. If you have family or friends who give holiday gifts, let them know the children need clothes, a library card, zoo pass, or money toward a larger purchase. My children frequently use holidays to give each other funds toward upcoming camps or mission trips.

Sometimes we allow ourselves to be loved. One of the most loving gestures I've received occurred when I moved to my new home. Two of my grown daughters and their friends traveled all day to spend three days doing for me the things I could not do for myself. They installed appliances, wired lights and ceiling fans, hung curtains and mirrors, fixed garage door openers and car fuses.

Organizations you participate in such as your church, 4-H, or Civil Air Patrol may offer scholarships for training or camps for you and your children. There are funds just waiting for someone to use them.

To supplement and stretch a budget, Denise researched community groups that distributed groceries and there were several months when I needed that service. Living in the northern Midwest where winter temperatures linger in the teens, she connected with a group that provided warm winter coats for her children. She sought out community supplements for her heating bills and shared this information with other single moms.

Develop co-ops to help each other tackle large projects. Occasionally I coordinate with another mom to trade weeks getting projects done at each other's homes. When our basements required organizing, Ann and I did it together. I went to her home for several hours one week and we decluttered her spaces. The following week she came to mine and helped me. In short order we had accomplished our projects and had a good time doing it. I've done the same with ladies when we wanted to get our yards spruced up. The work goes faster and is pleasant when done with a friend.

Trade services. I traded lawn equipment I no longer used to a landscaping guy for two months of lawn mowing. I traded furniture for help sorting and packing. It was worth it. Two moms swap math tutoring for art and English lessons.

Teaching our children to earn and manage their own money is a huge part of parenting. It is vital that they learn at home how the world works. People get paid for the work they do. Children can earn money by working for it. Whether children earn funds by raking the neighbor's leaves, shoveling snow, babysitting, playing music at rest homes, or picking produce at a farm, the next step is managing their income.

I'm a fan of the three-jar system. Ten percent of everything my children bring home goes into the Jesus Jar. That is their tithe and the children give this to the church and to additional projects they choose, from sponsoring a child locally or overseas, Operation Christmas Child, and Remedy.fm.

While they are young and at home, 40 percent goes into their savings jar and 50 percent is for spending. Early on, I take each child to the bank to open a savings account. They like seeing the amount increase and whether they add forty cents or forty dollars, any deposit is a good deposit.

Once a child begins driving, I like them to have a cell phone to let me know when they arrive and when they leave. I help them open a checking account as they will be making car repairs and putting fuel in the tank. Once that is rolling along with good addition and subtraction in the checkbook register, it's time to open a credit card account. I add the child to my credit card account and give them a card of their own with a small limit. We work together to manage the card, noting what will be charged (usually gas), managing the monthly payment, and accruing points. By this time some Internet orders typically go on the credit card, whether athletic shoes, equine supplies, or instrument strings. We get the chance to do that together, too.

Learning to wisely manage a savings, checking, and credit card are tools I want my children to learn while they are at home. This is an opportune time to look over car insurance rates, cell phone costs, medical expenses, utilities, as well as rent and mortgage estimations. It gives our children a healthy preparation for what lies ahead as they make choices for the future they want.

I do not mean that we dump our financial worries and concerns on our teens. It is not good that children should worry about money. Nor should they worry about whether they will be cared for by their parent. They are secure when they know how much they can spend.

"Today we're sticking to the dollar menu," I'll tell the children when that's what the budget allows. Other days I let them know we can be more extravagant. "Order whatever you want."

When shopping for groceries or clothes, I let them know the budget and they make great decisions. When a request is beyond the budget, I reply, "Not today and thanks for asking." Other times I might say, "Add it on the shopping list. We'll get it next time we shop."

Items and opportunities come along regularly that line up with someone's dreams. My response is, "Let's see how we can make that happen." We brainstorm mechanisms to make the dream reality.

One benefit to instructing others is what we learn in the process. As we go over these financial principles and structures with our children and teens, we become better acquainted with the information ourselves. Now that several of my children are adults, they also share great information with me regarding services and rates they use.

When you don't know what to do in a financial situation, seek wise counsel. Rather than spill your worries to just anyone, prayerfully consider those who are financially successful or trained in that area. Most people are happy to help outline your options. Take notes. Then make an educated choice. The choice is always yours and it is one of your most powerful tools. Even if you make a second-best decision, you will learn from it and that has value. Trust yourself to learn and to make great decisions.

 Those who trade liberty for security have neither.
John Adams

◁ Look Back

Take stock of your finances. Put together a working budget.

▷ Move Ahead

Where do you dream of being financially? What steps can you begin today to achieve your financial goal? A good first step is from every pay period, put 10 percent toward tithe—that's living in abundance— and put 10 percent in your savings. Budget to live on the rest. Increase these percentages regularly.

> May God give you of heaven's dew and of earth's richness—an abundance of grain and new wine.
>
> GENESIS 27:28

CHAPTER 21

FIT THE GLASS SLIPPER

Am I ready to date again?

People travel to wonder at the height of mountains, at the huge waves of the sea, at the long courses of rivers, at the vast compass of the ocean, at the circular motion of the stars; and they pass by themselves without wondering.

ST. AUGUSTINE

My fifteen-year-old son was appointed designated driver. Preop instructions restricted intake of food or fluids twelve hours prior and specified I drink twelve ounces of a horrible concoction that promised to elicit the emptying of my bowels. True enough, I was clean inside and out in the predawn hours as my son drove me to the hospital where a doctor from the urology group would blast a pesky kidney stone into easily passable gravel.

After registering, I was x-rayed again and had to fill more tubes with blood for tests. My clothes were exchanged for an immodest wrap the nurse called a gown.

"Gown?" I complained in my best Carl Hurley imitation. "This is an apron. My son wears something like this when he barbecues in the backyard."

Adorned in the timeless hospital attire, I was propped up in a rolling hospital bed and my son was invited back into the room until it was my turn to go down the hall to surgery.

"One last thing." The nurse held out a plastic cup. "We need a pregnancy test."

"No we don't."

"Policy," the nurse informed me.

"Trust me. I'm not pregnant."

My son took a step back.

"You're childbearing age," the nurse countered.

"I'm single. I've been single for several years. And even before that . . ." I could see my son retreating into the room's far corner.

"The doctor has had two instances when the woman was unaware she was pregnant," the nurse explained.

"You have to have sex to get pregnant. I know. I'm a mother of seven and I know how those things work." I glanced at my son. His eyes were wide. This was not only uncomfortable but was too much information for his teen thought process.

"Just collect a urine sample in the cup."

I sat forward. "I'm not paying for a test I don't need."

"Mom, she's just doing her job." My son's voice came from his corner. "It won't hurt to . . ."

From behind the nurse, in bustled a doctor in waistless surgical scrubs. Her blonde hair was pulled back from a pretty face. The nurse quickly stepped back, giving precedence to the physician.

"I'm Dr. Jean." She thrust forward a well-manicured hand sporting long, blood-red nails. "I'll be doing your anesthesiology."

I accepted the businesslike handshake. "I'm not taking your pregnancy test."

The doctor looked at the nurse who nodded and then receded further into her corner.

Dr. Jean regarded me. With the nurse in one corner and my son ensconced in the opposite corner, the scene resembled a prize-fight where coaches waited for the heavyweights to duke it out in the center of the arena.

"I'm not married, not seeing any men, nor has there been a star in the east for the past two thousand years," I listed. "It's physically impossible for me to be pregnant."

Patient and physician stared at each other. Homemaker and power woman played chicken in a standoff. Who would flinch first? The room was quiet but the air was charged.

"Very well," Dr. Jean said at last. "We'll wave the rabbit test."

"Rabbit test?" my son asked in a stage whisper.

"We'll talk about it later," I answered.

My son was outfitted with a buzzer and sent to work on his homework in the waiting room. The doctor would buzz him when the procedure was finished. At that time, she would give him postop instructions since I wouldn't be in much condition to remember directions.

"Not that she'll obey them anyhow," my son said.

I was wheeled into surgery and Dr. Jean began an IV. "Think of a nice dream," she instructed.

"My book is on the New York Times best-seller list." I felt a pleasant, fuzzy sleepiness spread through my body.

The anesthesiologist leaned close to my ear. "Your book is being made into a blockbuster feature movie."

"I like that better." And that was the last thing I remembered until recovery.

I'm a fermata, hold me.

T-shirt

Contrary to what people tell me, I have been able to live without sex for a decade, hence the story above. Don't get me wrong, sex is wonderful in the context of a loving marriage relationship and that would be my first choice. But to those who justify that humans can't live without their "needs being met," which is code for having sex, I beg to differ. So does God in his Word. Sex outside of marriage is called fornication. Sex with anyone other than your spouse when you are married is called adultery. It is sin.

In the same way we instruct young people to wait until they are married to enjoy the sexual union, single people like me are called by God to remain pure. Like any other temptation, this is one I must choose to resist.

Coming out of a broken relationship, two things happen. We are often eager to get into another relationship, and people around us are eager for us to get into another relationship. On a personal level, it feels odd to be unattached. Alone. A single in a couple's world. If someone found us attractive, it would certainly boost our wounded self-esteem. It would soothe those burning feelings of rejection.

This period of desperately desiring to be in relationship is real and it is powerful. As one woman put it, all men look the same and they all look good.

Those around us want us to find a relationship quickly for two reasons. They believe it will alleviate our pain over the end of this relationship. And it appears to be the answer to solving the awkward issue of getting together and doing things when most folks are a couple of some sort and you and I are definitely single.

Everyone is an example of what to do and what not to do. After watching lots of people frantically shop for another relationship to pop into so they can short-circuit the necessary and beneficial work of healing and becoming a whole person, I recommend the road less traveled.

Get emotionally healthy first. The rule of thumb is that this process requires you to remain single for one year per every four you were married. Don't date for at least one year. Get comfortable not needing another. Consider raising the children in a focused, balanced, loving single-parent home.

Fresh out of her marriage, a business associate went online to meet someone. "How about you?" she asked. "Found anyone new?" "Not looking," I replied. "I'm getting my private pilot's license." Her jaw dropped. "I never thought about doing something like that."

The ratio of men to women isn't encouraging for women. "Face it," my sister-in-law honestly observed, "at your age the good men are all taken. Anything left is either divorced with his own baggage or there's a reason why he's not taken."

Singles groups often look like dating services. Participants dance around each other hoping to match up or at least get a date. Since single was not my identity, I didn't plug in. My friends who have used dating services said the conversations move along quite nicely until the subject of children comes up. "Get real," one friend stated. "Anyone late twenties or older is going to have children. The men have children too, they just left them with their ex-wives."

Another little-addressed issue is that we must be ultra vigilant about who we allow to come into contact with our children. Boyfriends, stepdads, stepbrothers, and their extended family and friends don't have familial feelings toward our children. I know of too many cases where these men were sexually attracted to the daughters of the women they were dating. Many daughters have a huge need for male approval since their dads exited and these lovely young ladies don't have the maturity to discern the difference between healthy attention and selfish motives.

It is our job to protect our children. Women often pretend they are unaware of what is going on right under their noses when in reality they know something is amiss. Tragically, I've seen it happen over and over again. Never should my need for a man in my life cause me to compromise the safety and purity of my children.

It's normal to miss being loved and being in love. Recognize the tendency to think another relationship will be your savior. Only Jesus Christ can be your Savior. Having chosen to grit my teeth and put one foot in front of the other and wade through that period when I would have preferred the comfort and ease of retreating into a new relationship, I'm glad I made that investment into myself and into my family. At the time of this writing, I have been single for nine years. A natural team player, this is not what I would have chosen. I would have chosen the happily ever after with prince charming, thank you very much.

Yet, I have finally reached the place where I am comfortable in my skin, making decisions, and interacting with people. My confidence is growing and I'm discovering a freedom in my individuality. I come and go as I like and enjoy life. I'm a whole person. There is stability in my home. The children and I have a solid collection of friends we are authentic with.

One woman was a single mom with five children when she met a man she fell in love with. He had two children of his own. My friend carefully observed that she had a very different parenting style than he did. "I felt my children had been through enough," she related. "To give them the most consistency, I dated this man until all my children were grown. Then we married."

Prior to dating, assemble a list of what character traits are important to you. If honesty is foundational to your relationships, put that at the top of your list. If financial freedom is a priority, mark it down. Here is a sample list for the man I'm anticipating:

Loves the Lord Jesus Christ
Noble like the Scarlet Pimpernel
Brilliant
Wealthy
Adores me
Adores my children
Personally responsible
Bold
Courageous
Generous

Abundant
Joyful
Laughing
Fun
Honest
Open and vulnerable
Genuine
Physically fit
Sexy and sexual
Enjoys deep and long lasting relationships with family and
    friends
Invests in people
Travels
Adventurous
EnCOURAGEs me
Invests his life in significant, world-changing work
Respectful
Honoring
Faithful
Trustworthy
Truthful
Conversational
Learning and growing
Clear about his purpose and lives on purpose
Deep thinking
Intellectual
Hey, all I want is the perfect man.

 At some point, your heart will tell itself what to
do.

Achaan Chah

One of my favorite love stories belongs to my friend Kathi . . .

Immediately upon giving birth to her fifth child, Nelma's arms were empty. The hospital staff whisked away the baby before she could see him.

"I want to see my son," Nelma insisted.

"You need to understand, there are problems with the baby." The doctor explained that Nelma and her husband should consider an institution for their newborn.

"I want to see my son," Nelma repeated.

So the new bundle of babe was brought and placed in his mother's arms. Nelma smelled the sweet new baby smell of him; she cooed to the little boy and cradled him to her heart. Then, ever so carefully, she unwrapped his blanket. There lay her infant, born without legs, his hands and arms not fully developed. Nelma took it all in, caressed his soft new skin, and gazed into his trusting eyes.

"Oh." She smiled softly. "Is that all?"

And so Jerry went home with his mother to the welcoming arms of his family. There were struggles along the way as there are for all families, yet Nelma continued to love her children and cover them with prayer. The middle of seven children, Jerry was treated like everyone else in the family with the exception that there was no chair at Jerry's place at the dinner table to allow for his wheelchair. When it was Jerry's turn to wash the dishes, he washed the dishes.

When a man from the circus came to ask if Jerry could be part of their freak show, Nelma and her husband took the man by the scruff of his neck and threw him out of their home. "Jerry is not a freak," Nelma informed the visitor. "Jerry is our son."

Years later Jerry prepared to move away to college. A friend from church, Barbara was overjoyed that Jerry would attend the same campus where her daughter, Kathi, was enrolled. "Be sure to look her up when you get there," Barbara said.

Nearly a year later Kathi made an impulsive trip home. In the familiar surroundings of her mother's living room Kathi's confused emotions exploded into tears. "Mom, Jerry wants to marry me. I know he loves me and I love him. But Mom, Jerry doesn't have any legs. Can you marry someone without legs?"

Barbara's arms and calm voice encircled her grown daughter. "Honey, since you were young I have prayed for just the right husband for you. I prayed he would be a thoughtful, compassionate man. I prayed your husband would be strong in character and integrity, that he would be a leader in his home, and that he would provide well for you and your children. I prayed your future husband would know God, that he would be an honest, hard worker, that he would love you and be a tender life's partner. I prayed you would be best friends as well as husband and wife."

Barbara paused to lift Kathi's chin so their eyes met. "But Kathi, I never prayed for legs."

With the blessing of their parents, Jerry and Kathi were married. Jerry and Kathi had five beautiful children, every other one has red hair like their mother.

One day Jerry and Kathi's oldest daughter invited her school-age friend to come for dinner. Partway through her hot dog, the guest turned to her young hostess and reported, "Your dad doesn't have any legs."

Anna paused, peered under the dining table to study her dad parked in his wheelchair. Returning upright, she regarded her friend. "Your dad doesn't have a wheelchair."

A younger sister was learning in school about people with special needs. She came home from class one day and asked, "Mom, do we know anyone with disabilities?"

The beauty of Kathi's story is that it did not look the way she thought it would look. Our story didn't turn out the way we thought it would and it is not over. Though it may look different than we anticipated, you and I can still live happily ever after.

Dating is about first becoming friends. Develop same sex friendships, your core inner circle group. When meeting men, I believe it is pertinent that we don't compromise our reputation. For our sake and for our children, we are to avoid the appearance of evil.

Any man who is not considerate of my reputation and protective of my purity is not worthy of my time. No date should be asking for, or pressuring me for sex. It is not his right. If a relationship is not respectful and loving without the sex, it certainly won't be with sex.

Over lunch a friend confided, "This man really liked me. He wrote me beautiful letters every day. When we went out, we had sex. I thought it would be fun. But I haven't heard from him since."

As a Christian, you and I are daughters of the King. We are princesses. Royalty. Biblically we are joint heirs with God's only son, Jesus Christ, saved and redeemed, the temple of the Holy Spirit. Our name is written in the Lamb's book of life, and you and I are destined for eternal life. Culturally as women we have the right to vote, get a higher education, earn an income, have a career, own property, manage a business, employ others, and travel. You and I have the right to expect and demand honorable treatment from those around us including potential romantic interests.

You and I have permission to dress modestly, comfortably, and attractively simultaneously. I don't have to dress suggestively to get a guy's attention or prove I am sexy. We don't have to prove anything to anyone. Loved by God, we are enough.

You have permission not to have a man in your life at every moment. You have permission not to be anyone's all-in-all, not to have to keep the universe functioning, not to be anyone's savior. That job is already taken by Jesus Christ.

"It is for freedom that Christ has set us free. Stand firm, then, and do not let yourselves be burdened again by a yoke of slavery," says Galatians 5:1. With our identity secure in Jesus Christ, we are no longer slaves to our bodies, our singleness, our career, our friends, our heritage, or our ex-spouse. We are free to run into the welcoming arms of the Lord and call, "Abba Father."

When our date exercises self-control and is more concerned with our well-being than with his own desires, then he has the winsome characteristics of Boaz. The foundation of an excellent relationship is respect, honor, and integrity. Love is an added bonus. But without respect, honor, and integrity, there is nothing but toxicity and control.

When I was a tweener, both my parents remarried. Neither parent told me of their plans or invited me to be a part of their life-changing event. In both cases, I discovered I had a stepparent well after the fact. In both scenarios, I felt like the dangling participle left from their ill-fated marriage that neither wanted to remember or claim as they hurriedly embraced their new life. There was no sense of family. For me there was no belonging. I felt the sting of disrespect for a long time.

In contrast, after a respectful two-and-a-half year courtship, John wanted to marry my daughter. Prior to proposing, he met with me and each of her siblings to ask permission. Coordinating one-on-one meetings with every family member, including the youngest who was nine years old, required driving long distances when a couple of siblings were at summer camp and the older ones lived and worked a distance away. It took a week for John to meet with everyone. We pelted him with questions about his intentions and plans, his feelings, finances, and his relationship with the Lord. John was accountable and graciously accepted feedback from each encounter.

"This may be the most important question," I said after ninety minutes of other discussion.

He braced himself and leaned forward. "Okay."

"How do you feel about a very opinionated mother-in-law?"

Because Holly loved her family and John loved Holly, he quickly came to love who Holly loved. Because John built friendships with the people Holly loved, we knew his character and we observed first-hand how he treated his beloved. John displayed high honor for her and for each of us. It was a delight to unanimously welcome him into our family. The newlyweds planned the wedding exactly the way they wanted it and populated the ceremony with their favorite things including all of their family members.

"I watched you work harder for Holly than for anything else in your life," John's younger brother and best man toasted at the reception. "I'm proud of you, John."

Similarly, my neighbor Carolyn's love interest easily included her preschool-aged daughter in their dates. He gently built an easy rapport with the little girl and she was a prominent part of their wedding ceremony. Now married with children of her own, that child knew from the beginning she was valued and secure in a nurturing family.

A woman should never be in a place where she must choose between her children and a man. A man who loves and honors me will also love and respect my children. If your children, your horse, or your dog do not care for a man you are seeing, seriously consider their honest opinions. Horses and dogs don't lie.

Situations vary significantly. Some estranged parents remain strong in their parenting roles. Others disappear. Some chaotically come and go. A stepdad is exactly that. He will not replace a father. But a quality man can be like a father. He can be a beneficial, loving, and nurturing addition to the lives of children.

What are you looking for in a man?

> Devotion to God
> Honesty
> Protects your reputation and his
> Is interested in the things that are important to you
> Gets to know your heart
> Values your opinions
> Treats you with value

During the get-to-know you process:

+ Do see each other in a variety of settings: with friends, family, co-workers.
+ Don't only see each other when you are alone and looking your best on a date.
+ Do get to know each other for two years. The first year is the

honeymoon period. The second year is often when the masks go down, revealing a more genuine person.

+ Don't pretend you are someone you are not. If you don't really enjoy the hobbies he does but enjoy being with him, be honest.
+ Do ask trusted family and friends what they see in this person.
+ Don't ignore concerns of trusted family and friends. Nor should you make your decision solely based on their advice.
+ Do measure your relationship by how much each of you grow in your relationship with God.
+ Don't give up dreams, interests, and relationships with friends and family to be completely devoted to your boyfriend.
+ Do remember no one is perfect but never tolerate poor or disrespectful behavior.

Here are red flags that send me running in the opposite direction:
+ Anger
+ Smothering
+ Focus on the physical aspect of the relationship
+ Addictive behaviors (alcohol, spending, girl watching, drugs, pornography, computers, television, movies—anything that controls him and takes the place of God in his life)
+ Disrespectful to his mother, sisters, waitress, and other women
+ Uncomfortable making eye contact
+ Secretive
+ Manipulative
+ Disrespectful of your boundaries (One friend described how her date pushed himself past her to tour every room in her home. She felt violated by his lack of respect.)
+ Bulldozes through your "no"
+ Unhappy
+ Critical
+ Places responsibility for his emotions on others ("You made me . . .")

+ Unable to remember blocks of his childhood (This can be a typical survival response to abuse. If it is not faced and dealt with, the behavior comes out sidewise and adversely affects family members.)

It is perfectly normal for a woman to long for a life's partner. It is also perfectly normal for you and I to have high standards. To refuse to settle for second best. I propose that in the process of following your dreams and developing your gifts and talents, you will find fulfillment in pursuing your full potential in Christ. And as a whole and healthy person, you will attract another whole and healthy person. Then the relationship you create will be based not on need and dependency, but on the assurance that you are together because the foundation is solid.

And there are some noble stepfathers out there. Men who have room in their hearts for a woman and her children. My mastermind partner Lisa married a second husband who wholeheartedly embraced her and her five children. This gentle man wanted a family.

"One of our children is hers, one is mine, one is adopted, and one is ours," a stepdad told me. "But I can't remember which is which." In their family, the only thing that matters is that they are all a family and they belong together.

My favorite stepdad is Joseph of the New Testament. This man married a girl who was pregnant and not with his child. He left his family home in Nazareth, gave up his lucrative carpentry business, and traveled to live in a foreign country for many years to protect Mary and the child, Jesus.

When we are tempted to be jaded against men who have lived below their potential, it is important to remember and to remind our children that there are some great men out there.

 In a world where we're encouraged to do it "if it feels good," the Bible addresses that which is holy and that which is sinful. Scripture never leaves us with a bewildered look on our faces, wondering about the issues of life. It says, "This is the way to walk; do not walk there." It tells us straight. It provides the kind of solid foundation you and I need.

Charles Swindoll, *The Living Insights Study Bible*

◁ Look Back

For two years, attend events as a single person. Learn to interact authentically with others. Enjoy being you. One is a whole number.

▷ Move Ahead

What have you always wanted to do? Get your pilot's license? Dance? Scuba dive? Tour Europe? Cruise Greece? Read the classics? Get a degree? Replace those serviceable curtains you've hated for decades? Invite the Lord to be your date and do it.

A poet looks at the world
the way a man looks at a woman.

WALLACE STEVENS

CHAPTER 22

ADVENTURES IN WONDERLAND

Can I live in joyful abundance?

> Music expresses that which cannot be said
> and on which it is impossible to be silent.
>
> VICTOR HUGO

Dog lovers and cat lovers have long debated which is truly man or woman's best friend. Having had a half-dozen-plus-one children, I know from experience that where there are children, there are pets. And where there are pets, among the horses, pigs, goats, chickens, doves, and goose (yes, just one), there will be dogs and cats.

More than once, I have scratched the dog behind the ears, jumped in the car, and sped off, only to make it as far as the mailbox. Realizing someone left something essential behind, I turn the car around, drive back up the driveway and—even if I was in a hurry and ignored the dog as I left earlier—the loyal pooch greets me as if I am the center of the universe. Every time. Without fail. With tail wagging and happy whimpers, the dog gives his whole spirit to welcoming me home though I've only been away for forty-five seconds.

A dog is the only thing on earth that loves you more than he loves himself.

Josh Billings

The cat is a completely different story. The cat can ignore me for days. Someone brilliantly explained the phenomenon this way. In the beginning of time the dog observed how the mother of the family fed and cared for the dog and the dog concluded, "Wow, she feeds me and provides for my needs; therefore she must be god."

The cat, on the other hand, observed the same woman caring for the cat and deducted, "This human feeds me and cares for my needs; therefore I must be god." Cats were once worshipped in Egypt, a fact they have never forgotten.

A dog is the visual aid for giving 100 percent. Someone noted that the reason a dog has so many friends is that he wags his tail instead of his tongue. It was a wake-up call when I compared myself to the dog and saw he was the one who was living full out. For a long time, that was the opposite of how I lived life. As I speak at conferences and interview people, I see that living safe and small is common in people who have been held back and emotionally wounded.

Dogs hold nothing back. They love their owners unabashedly and unashamedly.

"I came that they may have life, and have it abundantly," declares the Lord in John 10:10 (NASB). God intended for us to live full and abundant lives.

Now.

Today.

What is in our hand to do? What has God given us as building blocks for this new life? What are the successful strategies others have employed? Can we still make a significant impact on the world?

I thought I was bold and brave, at least capable and responsible, until I was in a room full of people and we were challenged to cross the room from one side to the other. Simple enough, except each of us

REDISCOVERING YOUR HAPPILY EVER AFTER

had to cross in a different manner. For instance, if one person walked, no one else could use walking as a method to cross the room. As walking, skipping, running, hopping, walking backward, and the other obvious ideas were quickly employed, I pushed my way to the front of the line so I could get across before all the methods of room-crossing were used up and I was stranded. Left behind. Another example of others being successful while I missed out.

"Who scrambled to the front of the line because you were afraid of running out of mechanisms to cross the room?"

I raised my hand.

"That's a scarcity mentality," the facilitator explained. "Fear that there is not enough."

Fear that I was not enough.

That hour, two hundred people crossed the room using two hundred different methods. I've done this exercise many more times and now I run to the back of the line. Even as the last person, I always find a fresh way to travel to the other side of the room because I've learned that there is no limit. No scarcity. Several times I have been challenged to cross the room without using my hands or feet. What would you do? I can immediately think of a dozen ways to accomplish that goal.

As long as I thought there was not enough—not enough money, love, opportunities, education, careers, happiness, hope, fun, vacations, friends, (you fill in the blank)—I did not live full out. I limited myself even though God promised abundance.

Jesus Christ is our example of giving and living full out. He gave 100 percent of himself. God declares me a joint heir(ess) with Christ, and I have trouble leaving a decent tip for the waitress?

Shedding the scarcity mentality is like infusing my veins with jet fuel. I've given tips to people who've never received a tip before and it makes their day. Abundance is picking up the tab for others in a restaurant, funding kids to go to youth programs, contributing to scholarship programs, decluttering the stuff I hoarded and getting it back out into circulation for those who could use it.

After being hurt, my natural knee-jerk response is to pull in, withdraw like a hermit crab into a protective shell. That position yields the illusion that I am safer but it is impossible to live full out. When have you seen a hermit crab surfing? How often do we even see a hermit crab outside her shell? Not exactly the picture of an abundant life.

Ironically, tucked inside the small shell, I am lonely and I still get hurt. There is no protection against it but while trying to avoid the risk of feeling pain, I deprive myself and those around me of all that I truly am. I withhold giving my all in relationship with

> God
> Myself
> My children
> Grandchildren
> Family members
> Friends
> Neighbors
> Co-workers
> My work
> Church
> Community
> The world

I withhold compliments that can be freely scattered, favors that can be joyfully distributed, and love that can be unconditionally poured out.

When I shed the scarcity mentality that there is not enough and I am not enough, when I embrace the freedom of abundance and joy, I am able to be generous with genuine compliments, to smile and effortlessly do something extra along the way that brightens the day for someone else. A life of abundance is a life abundant with

> Embraces
> I love you
> I forgive you

Promises kept
Patient listening
Books read aloud to children without skipping pages
Time for others
Money to give
Grace toward myself

Abundance begins by being abundant with my self-talk. Studies indicate we say fifteen hundred words to ourselves per minute, some in pictures. Eliminate the three C's in your self-talk—criticism, condemnation, and complaints. Take out justifications. If that removes most of your self-talk vocabulary, we've already found the problem. Be tender with your words to yourself. Focus on compliments, acknowledge strengths, and dream big.

I can be generous in how I interpret events. What a relief to drop the self-inflicted judgment I attached to the event that sounds like, "If I had just . . ." "If I was enough . . ." "Because that happened I know about myself . . ." "I should have . . ."

My daughter reminds me, "Mama, don't *should* on yourself."

Instead I can cite what happened as an occurrence. Not proof of a judgment against myself.

 The average dog is nicer than the average person.
Andy Rooney

The scarcity mentality is particularly evident around people's money. Prior to an election a waiter engaged customers in conversation about their feelings regarding the economy. Without exception, those who thought the country was tanking did not leave a tip. Those who expressed hope that leaders would make good decisions and God was in control, left generous tips.

It's fun to tip people who don't usually receive extra. Often I know that a wife is wearily holding down the fort at home while her husband is traveling for work. I pad my check with instructions for him to take her to a relaxed dinner with my thanks for all she does. When I see military personnel, I shake their hand and thank them for their service on my behalf. At a restaurant, I pick up the tab for their meals. Not only am I grateful but any of them could be my son and I hope someone somewhere is doing the same for him.

When children stop by with Girl Scout cookies, 4-H geraniums, or an offer to wash my car, I'm an eager customer. What a simple way to encourage the younger generation and reward their efforts. If I don't need their product, I can donate to their group.

 If you pick up a starving dog and make him prosperous, he will not bite you; that is the principal difference between a dog and a man.

Mark Twain

"What did you do this week to change the world?" a friend periodically asks. It's a good question since my desire is to live a life of significance. Living in abundance includes doing something to benefit someone else. Though I didn't have the money to fund a foundation, adding my donation to that of others was collectively enough to provide college scholarships. Other significant ways to impact the world include sponsoring a child in music lessons, sports, or art class. Every time I do, I am passing on a significant gift that was given to my daughter.

Elderly and frail, a woman put a check in an envelope and addressed it to a teenager. She enclosed a note that read, "This will get you started."

A high school graduate, my oldest daughter dreamed of becoming a paramedic but lacked funds for the training. Until she opened her mail.

After completing the training, that paramedic serves her community around the clock. She is there for diabetic patients whose sugar gets out of control, for heart attack patients who need medication and a fast track to the hospital, and for those who find themselves tangled in vehicle accidents. She ministers to folks who call because of constipation, and the elderly who fall and can't get up by themselves. She knows those in her area that need regular medical attention and she shows up for callers who have never used emergency services before. She's there when it's a matter of life and death and she arrives when people telephone because they are lonely.

Though my dear elderly friend passed away, her investment into my daughter keeps on giving. Each time AmyRose saves a life, the gift is multiplied. Today AmyRose is an instructor, training a new generation of paramedics, thanks to a woman who wrote a check.

 What lies behind us and what lies before us are tiny matters compared to what lies within us.
Ralph Waldo Emerson

What is our prayer life like? Certainly God said to bring our petitions to his throne but much of our lack of abundance is in our viewpoint. What a positive change when my prayer life sounds like, "Thank you, Lord, for being my Source. For calming my anxious thoughts and comforting my heart. Thank you for your provision and protection. For strength, insight, and guidance. Thank you for loving me and my children more than I can imagine. Thank you for grace."

We can practice abundance now. Think of someone you choose to forgive. Do they deserve it? No. Did they ask for it? No again. Granting forgiveness is an abundant act you grant to them and to yourself.

Tuck aside money to give.

Focus on the positive in your life and center your conversation around that.

We are abundant with ourselves when we create. God is the universal creator. The first verse in the Bible says, "In the beginning God created . . ." (Gen. 1:1).

God created you with talents and abilities. What does it mean to cultivate creativity in your life? For me it means writing and connecting people who benefit each other. For my friend it means investing in historic buildings and restoring them to beauty in communities throughout the United States. For another friend, it means networking the various social-service groups in a large city to better assist the least of those in that community. The ways to be creative are as diverse as each of us.

Go ahead. Dare to dream. Dream big. Rest in the Lord as you cultivate something beautiful and amazing. Something just like you. Dreamers who hang pictures of their hopes in prominent places where they regularly see it report fast results between idea and reality. Sharing the idea with others often opens the door for networking with people who can facilitate your success. It creates a natural accountability when that other person regularly asks how you are progressing with your goal.

 Blessed are the single-hearted, for they shall enjoy much peace. If you refuse to be hurried and pressed, if you stay your soul on God, nothing can keep you from that clearness of spirit which is life and peace. In that stillness you will know what His will is.

Amy Carmichael

◁ Look Back

Be abundant with yourself. Give yourself the gift of a comfortably decluttered and organized home, office, and car.

▷ Move Ahead

Practice generosity. Have fun!

We are most like Christ when we forgive
and when we create.

PEGGYSUE WELLS

CHAPTER 23

Pinch of Pixie Dust

What future will I choose?

"Cheshire Puss," asked Alice, "Would you tell me,
please, which way I ought to go from here?"
"That depends a good deal on where you want to go,"
said the Cat.
"I don't much care where—" said Alice.
"Then it doesn't matter which way you go,"
said the Cat.

LEWIS CARROLL, *ALICE'S ADVENTURES IN WONDERLAND*

Close your eyes. Consider that your life is ending. Imagine your close friends gather around. You say good-bye to beloved family and loved ones. Stay in that place and notice what you are feeling. What do you wish you had done in your life? Where do you wish you had invested your time, talents, and passion?

Our lives are to be spent. Not to be saved. Each of us decides how we will invest our days. Today is an opportune moment to take stock and invest your life in pursuits that will outlive you. What is your five-year plan? Ten-year plan? The fifty-year plan? A five hundred–year plan?

History makers left a legacy that outlived them. Ruth, Deborah, Queen Esther, Mary the mother of Jesus, Queen Victoria, Golda Meier, Mother Teresa, George Washington, Patrick Henry, Abraham Lincoln, C. S. Lewis—there are plenty of names known and unknown who have had a significant impact on your life and mine today.

Life has a startling way of taking an unexpected turn, leaving us confused, insecure, and vulnerable. Standing at the crossroads, begin writing on the blank page of this chapter of your life. Embrace your new beginning.

How we invest our life is one of the most important decisions we make. Are you living on purpose? The adage goes that those who fail to plan, plan to fail. A study of college graduates showed that those who set goals and wrote them down had accomplished those goals when they returned to their class reunions. Graduates who set goals but did not write them down did not accomplish them. There is power in the written word even if it is the exercise of making a commitment to yourself by committing the words to paper.

Having trouble setting goals?

Write it down.

Often what we refuse to accept spotlights what we are called to do. Moses had a pile of excuses about why he could not do what God called him to do. "I stutter," was his justification. "Send my brother Aaron."

The only person who believes an excuse is the one serving it up. No one else is buying what you are selling any more than you believe the bologna others dish out to you. An excuse is nothing more than a well-crafted lie that no one believes except the person making it.

We come into the world with little more than our word. How we keep our word, our commitments, decides if we are a person of integrity who will leave the world with our word still intact. When a business associate commits to complete a project and doesn't follow through, and then blames others or circumstances, you and I both know they chose not to keep their commitment to themselves or to us.

What are you resisting? Examine your excuses. They probably point exactly to what God is calling you to do. You can do it easy or you can do it hard like Jonah. Suffering is optional.

Embracing your calling is like plugging your nose and diving straight into the rushing river of the Holy Spirit. Better yet, do a front flip. Somersault in. It's huge fun and a lot more satisfying than standing on the edge watching the river and the swimmers having a terrific time without you.

If you could do anything, regardless of money, time, abilities, or any other hindrances, what would that be? No matter how crazy, what desire burns deep in your heart? What do you yearn to do and be?

 Obstacles are those frightful things you see when you take your eyes off your goal.

Henry Ford

What do you want to be sure you do before the end of your life? What is it that you don't want to regret *not* doing? The time is now.

Keeping your eye on the goal, and not on *how* to get there, what step will you take toward your dream today?

Set goals in six areas: personal, career, spiritual, physical, relational, and financial. Include dates such as "I will have a three-month emergency savings account funded in twelve months." Attach celebrations and consequences to your goals. For instance, "When my savings account is funded in twelve months, I will celebrate by going to dinner with a friend. If my account is not funded in twelve months, I will clean my friend's house." Make sure your friend has a copy of your goal so she can encourage you because in this scenario, either way, it is a win for your friend.

I want to live my calling instead of bumping around wondering what my calling is.

"I don't know what I want to do," a lady told me. "The passion is beat right out of me." I suggested she begin a journal and write down insights into her soul, what she likes and what she doesn't like. She journaled her real feelings, the ones she had become accustomed to burying. Before long, she had an inspiring picture of herself.

An artist in Michigan purchased a cottage and let herself go as she decorated. That cozy dwelling was transformed into a multisurfaced canvas.

"What do you think my house looks like?" asked my mentor the first time she invited me to her home.

"Uniquely beautiful like you."

"But what does it look like?" Saundra pressed.

"Probably classic antiques," I guessed.

What I saw when I came through the front door still takes my breath away. Her country abode was a Christmas wonderland. The sparkling, ceiling-high Christmas tree was catalog-perfect skirted by a pile of brightly wrapped packages.

It was summer.

"Pick a gift," she invited.

My children and I starred dumbly at her.

She urged us closer. Gathered around the holiday tree, she distributed presents tagged with our name. Then we selected another from the unnamed but beribboned gifts. Of course, each item was just right.

"This is wonderful," I said. "But I don't understand."

"Christmas," she said, "is not just one time a year. Giving is not seasonal."

For over a decade, it is always Christmas at her home. My children call it the Christmas House. Every visitor who enters Saundra's home chooses a gift from under the decorated tree. It is Christmas in her heart, too. She is famous for sowing what she calls seed money. Monetary gifts tucked into pockets and envelopes that she gives and encourages the recipient to pass on.

Years ago, as a single mom raising five children in a tiny Midwest town, Saundra barely kept food on the table. She turned to Scripture for answers. "In His Word, God gave keys for living," she said. "One of those keys is give and it shall be given unto you."

Saundra began giving fifty dollars and a hundred dollars to someone at her annual family reunion, a gathering of extended relations and friends. Today she gives three such gifts. "When I started I didn't have the money to give," she admitted. "The gas and electric bills needed to be paid and I needed to purchase a baby gift and a Mother's Day gift. In my prayer time, the Lord seemed to ask what my need was *today*. My need today was to begin the seed idea. I couldn't make my weekly paychecks go where I needed them to go so the Lord encouraged me to give, in addition to my tithe, one paycheck per month to him. By the end of the week I had the gifts I needed and the bills were paid. The year I began giving, my business grew from three thousand dollars yearly to enough to provide for my family and pay off my home."

Similarly, putting feet to the Gaither Vocal Band song, *Give It Away*, five people are randomly selected at Gaither concerts to receive two hundred dollars each in seed money to plant in their communities. The stories come back of transformed lives.

Walt Disney dreamed of a park where adults could have fun with their children. Previously, a parent took a child to a park and watched them have fun. Since it had not been done before, Walt did not have a model to follow. He risked everything he had in terms of finances and energy to launch Disneyland. Today Disney is synonymous with their tagline, the happiest place on earth. Have you been there lately? Crowds of families are drawn to pack the parks every day. Disney is one of the largest private employers in the nation.

When he personally provided a four-year college scholarship, Walt Disney was instrumental in launching the career of writer/producer Ken Wales. Likewise, Ken mortgaged his house multiple times to bring the story of *Christy* to television. Following his passion, Ken realized his dream when *Christy* became the most watched television show on the Easter Sunday when it debuted. Ken realized another dream when the story of William Wilberforce became a feature film titled *Amazing Grace*.

 You got to be very careful if you don't know where you're going, because you might not get there.

Yogi Berra

Have a knowing-where-you-want-to-go kind of a day!

 Think of standing next to a quiet pool of water. Did I hear someone say, "Cannonball!"?

Source unknown

◁ Look Back

What excuses do you have for not moving forward in life? What do those excuses illuminate about what you could be doing? Practice saying to yourself, "No excuses." Watch how your conversations improve and people enjoy being with you when you shed tiresome justification.

▷ Move Ahead

Draft a plan for your future. Use your plan as a compass. Each year, make course adjustments to your life plan as you accomplish hopes and dream new dreams.

On a large, colorful poster board glue pictures of things you dream about. Money and time are not factors to consider. For instance, if you want to travel, include photos of the destinations you want to visit. If you want to learn to fly, put up a picture of a plane. If you want a relationship, add that to your collection. The sky is the limit. Hang your dream board where you will see it every day. One friend turned a bedroom wall into a large dream board.

Label the top of a paper, "In One Year," and free flow your thoughts about where you want to be in one year. Do the same for Five Years, Ten Years, Twenty Years, and Five Hundred Years. Having a five hundred–year plan helps you do things today that will positively impact the world in a way that outlives you. The Bible and our history books are filled with people who did just that. You can too.

From your plans, choose three goals to focus on. Three dreams that make your eyes light up and your heart quicken with excitement. Post those on a note card where you will see them every day.

Each day, write down three action steps that will move you toward your goals.

Do the action steps first.

Once a week write in the most important items of the upcoming seven days on the calendar to make sure they get priority attention.

Monthly, schedule priority items in priority slots.

Yearly, celebrate your progress and set your goals for the upcoming year.

> The major reason for setting goals is to *compel* you to
> become the person it takes to achieve them.
>
> JIM ROHN, *7 STRATEGIES FOR WEALTH & HAPPINESS*

CHAPTER 24

HAPPILY EVER AFTER

Could I make a difference?

We make a living by what we get.
We make a life by what we give.

WINSTON CHURCHILL

I want you to know," my friend wrote, "how sorry I am about your situation. I happened upon the news over a year ago, but I didn't want to bring it up. You and your precious kids have been in my prayers since that time. I can't even imagine the hurt, pain, and devastation you've experienced."

This honest correspondence reminded me of an earlier event in my life. After my daughter died, my sister-in-law telephoned from another state. "I've been trying to get your brother to call," she apologized, "but he doesn't know what to say."

My brother's discomfort and bewilderment over the loss of my daughter, like my friend's feelings over the loss of my marriage, is common. What *can* you say to soothe someone who is suffering an inconsolable loss?

The truth is that our finest moments are most likely to occur when we are feeling deeply uncomfortable, unhappy, or unfulfilled. For it is only in such moments, propelled by our discomfort, that we are likely to step out of our ruts and start searching for different ways or truer answers.

M. Scott Peck, *Abounding Grace*

God does not expect us to be experts but he does call us to come alongside one another during the darkest hours. We have experienced a tremendous sadness. We know what that feels like. Now it is our turn to comfort others. Whether it is the loss of their marriage partner or another traumatic event, how can you and I be the hands of Jesus to someone who is suffering?

A crisis can destroy someone or it can make that person stronger. Deeper. The turning point comes in how we face the crisis. How we face the crisis often depends on what kind of support we receive.

You have faced your own crisis. Some of us had terrific support. Some of us didn't. Either way, we have real life experience that could support another who faces their own crossroad. We also have compassion and empathy we probably didn't possess prior to this. Before my own divorce, when I encountered someone who was having marriage problems, my mental judgment was, "Hey, if you just do what the Bible says, you'll have a great marriage."

Yes. And no. There is no magic formula. Nor do I have any control whatsoever over the behavior of another. I struggle to make the necessary changes and improvements in my own behavior.

 If you can't get rid of the skeleton in your closet, you'd best teach it to dance.

George Bernard Shaw

It is never necessary for us to have our lives all in order before we help another. This myth is particularly destructive for single women. I've seen some churches and Christian schools strip a woman of her teaching position when she becomes divorced. I've seen this happen even in cases where the marriage ended because the husband chose to pursue an adulterous relationship. The wife feels like she is being punished for her husband's behavior. Does a man experience professional or social consequences for divorce? For women, such situations shatter an already fragile confidence and many of us accept the lie that we no longer have anything of value to share.

On the contrary, I encourage you to see how this unwanted event has equipped you to come alongside others who are in the midst of their own calamity. You know from your own experience that comfort comes from large as well as seemingly small gestures.

You have much of value to offer. Life is a team sport. Come off the spectator stands and jump into the game. Young and bored with life, author Bill Myers was challenged to say yes to whatever God asked him to do.

"I see so many people sitting comfortably on the bleachers, watching the game," he observed. Bill's life became a nonstop adventure when he jumped out of his seat, begged God to pick him, and ran into the game.

"The next thing I tried to do was out-give God," Bill said. "You can't out-give this guy!"

 Don't ask yourself what the world needs. Ask yourself what makes you come alive, and go do that, because what the world needs is people who have come alive.

Howard Thurman

Multi–Dove Award winners Bill and Gloria Gaither said a large part of their grand, worldwide adventure with the Lord happened because they "showed up every morning." God uses those who are willing and available. Gloria said she sets goals for the day and allows God to interrupt her with his plans.

People need hope more than advice. One woman shared, "When my dad died, I held it together until after the funeral. Then I fell apart. People tried to say the right thing, but there just aren't any right words. I felt the most comforted by one friend who simply cried with me."

Job would agree. When he lost his material wealth the same day that disaster claimed all ten of his children, friends offered endless advice and their own spiritualized explanations of the catastrophe. Job called them "miserable comforters" (Job 16:2). "For the despairing man there should be kindness from his friend; so that he does not forsake the fear of the Almighty" (Job 6:14 NASB).

The very idea of loss is uncomfortable and triggers awkward situations. After my friend's children were killed in a car accident, she noticed some people actually turned away when they saw her around town. We may need to get past our discomfort and fear if we are to be helpful. "The people I appreciated most," Barbara said, "were those who hugged me and said, 'I've been thinking of you.'"

 We may give without loving, but we cannot love without giving.

Amy Carmichael

At times we feel confused about how to help bereaved friends. The answer can be as simple as imagining ourselves in their painful shoes. When my neighbor's husband died, she was comforted by those who thought to walk with her in the church parking lot, who sat with her so she wouldn't be alone in her regular pew, and who invited her to lunch on an otherwise lonely weekend afternoon.

My friend Mary Ann is an expert comforter. "I don't understand," she said, "but I'm here to take every step of the journey with you."

Though she lives far away, she consistently found ways to be with me through phone calls, e-mails, and thoughtful gifts.

Since we know that nothing at all—neither the painful things in our life or even death—can separate us from the deep love of Jesus (Rom. 8:38–39), we can cling along with our hurting friend to that love, even as we fail to understand the why of the tragedy.

Time doesn't heal our wounds when we've had to say good-bye to a loved one; it coaches, tutors, mentors us in the delicate skill of living with that big gaping hole in our heart. Sharing the journey of grief helps. As Ecclesiastes 4:10 says, "If one falls down, his friend can help him up. But pity the man who falls and has no one to help him up!"

I can say from experience that the first year after losing a loved one or a longed-for marriage is particularly difficult, especially on those important dates. While outsiders quickly forget that someone significant is missing, holidays continually remind the bereaved that life is forever altered. You can comfort and show love to a still-grieving friend by simply making a telephone call or sending a note, flowers, or memorial gift. Don't be afraid that you're making things worse—your friend's thoughts are undoubtedly already on his or her loved one. If you are remembering the date, imagine how much more your friend is aware of the anniversary.

"Valentine's Day is single-awareness day," one single stated. On my first Valentine's Day as a single, Mary Ann celebrated me with a package containing tea, chocolate, and a book that reminded me that God was head-over-heels crazy in love with me.

What a consolation it was when friends invited me for dinner on my first Christmas Eve without my children. It was heartbreaking that on this family holiday the only person who was not included in the festivities was me—the wife and mother. Around my friend's dinner table that night were a collection of folks; two families and three of us singles. They had room enough in their home because there was room in their hearts.

Marriage anniversaries can be tough days for those who wanted to stay married. One woman's deepest heartbreak occurred the day her beloved husband married the woman he had left her for. To make the day even worse, she was alone while her school-age children attended the wedding, after which the newlyweds left for her dream honeymoon destination that he would never take her to. "I couldn't have survived," she recalled, "without my friends who came and stayed by my side that horrible day."

The story is told that the pride of a small town in Europe was their statue of Jesus in the village square. During World War II, the town was bombed. The townspeople collected the pieces of the destroyed statue and painstakingly did their best to re-create it. When they finished gluing the statue back together, the only pieces missing were the hands of Jesus. They placed a plaque at the base of the statue with this message:

Now we are the only hands that Jesus has.

We have an enormous opportunity to be the hands of Jesus that reach out and bring hope and encouragement to a hurting world. As we touch others who are in distress, we become a conduit connecting them with God's unfailing love. Romans 8:38–39 promises, "I am convinced that neither death nor life, neither angels nor demons, neither the present nor the future, nor any powers, neither height nor depth, nor anything else in all creation, will be able to separate us from the love of God that is in Christ Jesus our Lord."

Often the best comfort comes from one who has been there. "What are you going to do now?" I asked a friend after church the first Sunday her children were away visiting their father.

"Go home, I guess," she answered.

"Let's get a beer," I teased.

The absurd idea made her laugh for the first time in a long while. Actually, we went out for a milkshake. But I remembered how unfair life felt going home all alone the first Sunday my own children were away.

Past the seeker as he prayed came the crippled and the beggar and the beaten. And seeing them, he cried, "Great God, how is it that a loving creator can see such things and yet do nothing about them?" And God said, "I did do something. I made you."

Sufi teaching

We, of all people, understand the upheaval of a life in transition. We can expand our sphere of influence to include anyone traveling a journey of adjustment. What did you wish you had help with when you first became single? Finances? Legalities? Yard work? Babysitting? Did you long for invitations to be with people and have fun and laugh? Chances are, your experience won't be much different from someone else who is journeying through trials and tribulations.

I found myself with a section of my roof stripped and the spring rains approaching. A couple that had shingled their own roof several years earlier offered to spend a day helping me complete that back room. I ignored my fear of heights and we spent a full day like cats on a hot plywood roof. The few shingles that went on tar side up were mine but they assured me it was close enough for country. Soaking in a hot tub that night waiting for the ibuprofen to take effect, I was overwhelmed with gratitude for these precious people who helped me exactly where I most needed it.

Similarly, a young friend who was a peer of my college kids replaced a broken window and two faulty toilets. "I work for food," he said.

Some of the best gifts were the folks like that young college man who just stopped by to visit. Those who sat at my table and ate with us, played games with my children, gave a hand with household projects, invited us to events, and treated me and my children like we didn't have the plague merely because I was now single.

A note of caution as you walk with someone through a marriage crisis. It is possible to comment that a spouse's behavior is not respectful or lawful without resorting to character assassination. The situation of another is never license for you or me to vent residual contention and bitterness lingering from our own issues. Nor can we assume that what happened to us is what is happening to our friends. The outcome of their situation will be different. Their marriage crisis may end in reconciliation and they may live happily ever after. What delight to have been a support in a happy ending. Sometimes the happy ending looks very different because a woman decides she will no longer stay in an abusive situation. Either way, the decision belongs to the people in the crisis.

When women ask me pointed questions, I remind them that I can only share from my own experience, my research, and from what I've observed others go through. Usually what they truly want is for me to ask open-ended questions that help them clarify their chaotic confusion.

"What end result do you want?" I ask.

When these women are able to state their goals, then they can aim for the target.

Looking back, what I needed most in the worst of my turmoil was clarity in the confusion and a solid game plan. For too many of us, we are so blindsided that we sit like a rowboat without oars in the middle of a becalmed sea socked in by a pea soup fog. We need people to help us find a couple of oars and a compass. Not to set the course or do our rowing. We must do that for ourselves. It is our journey, after all.

Now that you are the helper, remember that there is a Mt. Everest of difference between supporting and rescuing. Rescuing is fixing someone's problem for him or her. Supporting is allowing them to fix their own problem. Rescuing is getting in my rowboat and rowing me to the destination you think is best for me. You arrive breathless and with sore arm muscles and I will complain about where I am. Supporting is giving me oars and a compass and asking me where I will row to.

We are called to daily mirror Jesus Christ by being his helping hands to a hurting world. As I received much-needed help, now I keep the gift going by giving to others. The critical piece in helping others is the ability to see and feel their pain. God consoles us so we can be links in God's chain of compassion to others.

 Praise be to the God and Father of our Lord Jesus Christ, the Father of compassion and the God of all comfort, who comforts us in all our troubles, so that we can comfort those in any trouble with the comfort we ourselves have received from God. For just as the sufferings of Christ flow over into our lives, so also through Christ our comfort overflows.

2 Corinthians 1:3–5

If I were a betting woman, I would bet you lunch out that each of us has a story or ten about people who left us more wounded than we were before they tried to help us. It is vital that our attempts to help are not packaged in judgment and opinions that leave people more devastated than they were before they encountered our help. When we come in contact with a person who is suffering, do we leave them feeling enCOURAGEd, or more wounded?

We, more than most people, know better than to assume that marriage relationships are fine. In a crisis, whether it is an ill child, a job loss, relocation, or loss of a loved one, two drowning people cannot save each other. Gently ask your friend how her marriage is holding up. You may be the one to help a couple seek appropriate counseling.

Here is what I've learned does *not* help:

1. Don't resort to clichés. Express something genuine like, "I'm sorry," even if it seems inadequate. Trite phrases like "God is using you to teach other people who are watching your example," rank up there with telling someone whose child died, "God must have needed

another angel in heaven or another flower in his garden." Both reduce God to a selfish, needy deity.

2. Resist saying, "At least you had those years together," or "At least you're young enough to marry again," or "At least you got the house," or "At least you have children." Minimizing someone's pain by saying *at least* insults the griever.

3. Don't assume it's too late to offer support. Long after others have moved on, your encouragement may be desperately needed. Grief can be a long process.

"It's been three months, haven't you moved on?" This is a common question. Perhaps three months is the time period those who are not grieving are comfortable allowing for those of us who are. But you and I know that while we may make great progress and be doing well at one moment, with the next phone call or attorney letter our world can turn upside down once again. Too often our situation involves getting over one grief only to be bulldozed by another.

4. Don't pressure someone to talk about their situation. Provide the opportunity by asking, "How are you?" If someone doesn't want to talk, just allow their "Fine," to be fine. If there is a need to talk, that question is enough to invite dialogue. When that happens, the best gift is to listen without interrupting.

5. Don't try to distract the griever with too much busyness. Grief cannot be walked around; it must be walked through.

6. Don't offer the well-meaning but vague, "If there's anything I can do, call." They won't. When a friend's child required critical surgery, her support group coordinated a prayer chain, meals, and sibling care. Make concrete suggestions like, "I'll be at the market today. What can I pick up for you?"

7. Don't say, "I know how you feel," even if you've faced a similar circumstance. Each relationship is unique with positive and negative nuances outsiders cannot comprehend. Instead, try phrases like "How do you feel about . . . ?" or "I imagine you feel . . ." which can demonstrate a desire to understand.

8. Don't use Scripture casually. To a person in mourning, even the encouragement of Romans 8:28 can sound like a platitude. Ask the Holy Spirit's guidance for comforting verses to share.

9. Don't expect people to grieve in a prescribed way or on a particular timetable. While the mourning process includes identifiable stages that are useful to understanding, be careful not to label or place expectations on the mourner.

Frequently we help from an area where we are already talented. If you enjoy cooking, double the recipe and drop off a hot dish. If you are often in your car, offer to run errands, drop off and pick up children, or take someone to appointments. One neighbor mows a woman's yard. Two women tutor kids with their homework and I will always be thankful for those times when a neighbor surprised me by plowing my long driveway after a snowstorm had left us snowed in. Though she lives states away, Cecelia helped me navigate the jungle of medical insurance forms. A professional in this arena, her assistance came naturally for her and was a tangible help to me.

Have a wonderful journey today. And every day!

 If you want to build a ship, then don't drum up people to gather wood, give orders, and divide the work. Rather teach them to yearn for the far and endless sea.

Antoine de Saint-Exupéry

◁ Look Back

Who in your circle is in crisis? What areas in your community could use your ideas to improve?

▷ Move Ahead

On a local level, come alongside a person or group where you can contribute your talents to support—not rescue—another who could use a helping hand. Expand your influence globally by getting involved with a group that makes a difference beyond what you can do by yourself.

> It is good to have an end to journey toward;
> but it is the journey that matters, in the end.
>
> URSULA K. LEGUIN

WHICH WAY TO MY HAPPILY EVER AFTER?

Saying good-bye to a marriage relationship truly is a tearing of flesh and heart. Saying good-bye to the family you dreamed of building together is a reason for deep grief.

Each day for one month, read one statement below and journal your thoughts and emotions. Putting one foot in front of the other, you will get through the desert of grief and enter the Promised Land of the next chapter of your life. Take pen in hand, and begin. One day at a time.

Time doesn't really heal all wounds.
Time merely teaches us how to live
with this gaping hole in our heart.

✦ ✦ ✦

Crisis wears many faces.
Crisis can look like the loss of a loved one,
the loss of a relationship,
the loss of a marriage, the loss of a job,

the loss of what is familiar due to relocation,
the loss of a dream.
A crisis is a turning point.
Yet while we are in crisis we often feel
powerless, hopeless, desperate, paralyzed.
Crisis can destroy us.
Or crisis can make us stronger.
It all depends on how we face the face of crisis.

+ + +

No one can avoid it,
go around it,
slide under it,
fly above it,
or swim below it.
Grief cannot be walked around,
it must be walked through.
One step at a time.
One day at a time.

+ + +

It seems like you had to say good-bye
before you had the chance to say hello.

+ + +

Life changed overnight.
This was so unexpected.

+ + +

Too often, tears are the only water in the dry desert of grief.

+ + +

There are many difficult decisions to make.

+ + +

No one can take away the pain
and few understand the depth of your grief.
Though the scars remain,
the open wound eventually heals.

+ + +

Swimming with the tide is easy.
Swimming against the tide increases your strength.

+ + +

When you feel like you are in the pressure cooker,
it's time to let off steam in a healthy manner.
Talk to a friend,
take a walk,
journal your honest thoughts,
scrub something until it shines.

+ + +

People often mean well but say the wrong things.
Listen to their hearts, not their words.

+ + +

Though the situation seems overwhelming right now,
may it soon open the door to opportunity.

❖ ❖ ❖

Someone may be willing to help carry the burden.
Maybe then it won't seem so heavy.

❖ ❖ ❖

Hope and encouragement are better than advice.

❖ ❖ ❖

Anniversaries of loss and grief
are annual reminders of our pain
and of how far we've come
on the journey to the other side of grief.

❖ ❖ ❖

Our own deep grief reminds us not to turn away
when we see others in pain.
We can cry with them. We can give a hug.
We can ask, "How are you?" and really mean it.

❖ ❖ ❖

Another who is grieving can be a companion
through the journey,
but may not be able to give comfort.
Two drowning people cannot save each other.

✦ ✦ ✦

Healing cannot be rushed.
It's harmful to tackle projects we're not ready for.
There are no deadlines for when we must be over it.

✦ ✦ ✦

When we are drowning in grief
it's okay to cry.

✦ ✦ ✦

We fear the waves of grief will overwhelm us.
Choose to ride through the powerful emotions now
so the unfinished process will not haunt the future.

✦ ✦ ✦

Being bitter about the loss only increases the pain.
We can be thankful for what we had,
for what we still have,
and for what the future holds.

✦ ✦ ✦

There is a whole world out there
just beyond the pain.
There is a whole world out there
in spite of the pain.
Go to a movie,
try a new restaurant,
visit a museum.

✦ ✦ ✦

When someone wants to talk
and we don't feel like it,
we don't have to.

✦ ✦ ✦

It helps to have a safe someone to talk to
when it's time to talk.

✦ ✦ ✦

It is surprising when close friends don't understand.
It is surprising when support comes
from unexpected sources.

✦ ✦ ✦

It's not comforting when someone says,
"At least you had those years together."
Or "At least you don't have to worry anymore."
At least we've learned not to tell another, "At least . . ."
We've learned to say, "I'm sorry."

✦ ✦ ✦

Cocooning is tempting.
Some alone time is good.
Balance it with time out and with others.
Say yes to many invitations.
We can't wait for someone to invite us out.
Invite someone else out for a milkshake or a concert.

✦ ✦ ✦

There is no aspirin for heartache.
Chocolate is medicinal.
So is tea.

✦ ✦ ✦

A stuffed teddy bear is something to hold onto.
A good book or video is for losing your mind
in something other than the pain.

✦ ✦ ✦

On the journey of grief
we will meet fellow travelers.
Perhaps we can walk a while together.

✦ ✦ ✦

Finally, brothers, whatever is true, whatever is noble,
whatever is right, whatever is pure, whatever is lovely,
whatever is admirable—if anything is excellent or
praiseworthy—think about such things. Whatever you have
learned or received or heard from me, or seen in me—put it
into practice. And the God of peace will be with you.
Philippians 4:8–9

NOTES

Chapter 6: Read the Story

1. Pat Palau and PeggySue Wells, *What to Do When You're Scared to Death* (Oxford, UK: Monarch, 2008), 137.

Chapter 8: Safe in the Brick House

1. See, for example, Barna Group, "New Marriage and Divorce Statistics Released," March 31, 2008, http://www.barna.org/barna-update/article/15 -familykids/42-new-marriage-and-divorce-statistics-released; and "Born Again Christians Just As Likely to Divorce As Are Non-Christians," September 8, 2004, http://www.barna.org/barna-update/article/5-barna -update/194-born-again-christians-just-as-likely-to-divorce-as-are-non -christians.

Chapter 9: A Pea Under the Mattress

1. Carolyn Koons, "Healing the Past and Moving On I–II." *Focus on the Family with Dr. James Dobson,* radio broadcast CD.
2. Robert Jeffress, *When Forgiveness Doesn't Make Sense* (Colorado Springs, CO: WaterBrook, 2000), 111.
3. Philip Yancey, *What's So Amazing About Grace?* (Grand Rapids: Zondervan, 1997), 137.

4. Lewis Smedes, *Forgive and Forget: Healing the Hurts We Don't Deserve* (New York: HarperOne, 1984), 108, 114.

5. Jackie Kendall, *Free Yourself to Love: The Liberating Power of Forgiveness* (Brentwood, TN: FaithWords, 2009), 21.

6. From Kendall, *Free Yourself to Love*, chapters 4–8.

7. Mary Ann Froehlich, personal conversation with author.